NIG

**D0120810**

NIGEL WILLIAMS is former producer of *Bookmark*
and currently producer of *Omnibus*. He has also
written three bestselling comic novels, including *The
Wimbledon Poisoner* and *They Came from SW19*.
Among his plays are *Sugar and Spice*, *Class Enemy*
and *Country Dancing*. He is married, with three
children, and lives in south-west London.

Nigel Williams

# TWO AND A HALF MEN IN A BOAT

First published in Great Britain in 1993 by Hodder and Stoughton Ltd
First published in paperback in 1994 by Hodder and Stoughton, a division of Hodder Headline PLC

*A Sceptre paperback*

**British Library C.I.P.**

Williams, Nigel
  Two and a half men in a boat. –
  New ed
  I. Title
  914.204

10 9 8 7 6 5 4 3 2 1

ISBN 0 340 60976 1

Printed and bound in Great Britain for Hodder and Stoughton, a division of Hodder Headline PLC, 338 Euston Road, London NW1 3BH.

To the hardworking men of the Inland Revenue Collections Division (Bradford and Wandsworth branches) without whose zeal and commitment this book would never have been written.[1]

---

[1] This dedication was suggested by Mr Robert McCrum of Faber and Faber who has pointed out that P.G.Wodehouse once dedicated a book to an accountant who saved him from a large tax bill. In case the reader should suspect this book was *only* written for the money (a suspicion McCrum probably intended his dedication to create) I offer the following alternatives:

1. For Brad Ziegmann, because he believed.
2. For Lou Mary-Ellen, Julian Barnes, Martin Amis, Ian McEwan and everyone at Viking, who beleived in this book before and after it was written. Thanks, guys.
3. In memory of Julian Schneider, who loved this park.
4. For my family, who no longer avoid me.
5. For Hunslett Greene – great teacher, great scholar.
6. For the ghost of Goethe, in whose shadow I toil.

The best-ever dedication, beating even the kind of log-rolling now almost obligatory for a certain kind of contemporary American writer, is probably Stephen Potter's: *For Phyllis in the hope that one day* God's *glorious gift of sight may be restored to her.*

# Preface to the First Edition

The charm of this book does not lie in its profundity or with the elegance with which it has been written. It will be read primarily because the events it describes did, in the main, actually take place. JP, Alan and Badger are all real. Especially Badger, who is sitting on my floor chewing pieces of paper as I write. My portrait of them however, bears little relation to how they actually are, and any eccentricities observable in the behaviour of the men and animals in the work that follows are entirely the product of the diseased imagination of the writer.

Wimbledon
September 1993

# One

*I am visited by the Inland Revenue – Sangfroid of wife – Importance of Colindale to accountants – Need to escape from financial ruin – Reluctance of Self to go on holiday – Similar diffidence with regard to adventure – Excellent advice from son – I resolve to undertake a journey.*

Until nine months or so ago I had never met anyone from the Inland Revenue. I assumed they spent their days in tall, faceless buildings, devising forms that were impossible to understand then sending them to distant parts of the country. I had difficulty imagining them doing anything not directly connected with tax.

If I had tried to visualise them at all I think I would have pictured men in suits and sober ties. Which is why, when my wife informed me there were two men from the Inland Revenue in my front hall, I was surprised to see that one of them was got up with the sort of effortful informality common among off-duty policemen.

Indeed, from the severity of his haircut and the size of his feet, this was what I took him to be. He was wearing a red shirt, a leather jacket and dark blue trousers and carrying the sort of clipboard used by the compères of quiz shows. He did not, however, have the look of a man about to offer me a microwave or a Ford Sierra. He had clearly got something on his mind. He was wearing a badge of some description which, if you had got close to it with a magnifying glass, might have told you what his name was. From this distance it looked as if he was called Drain – Mr Drain.

'Henry Nigel Williams', he said, 'my colleague and I are from the Inland Revenue.'

I do not like it when people use my full name. I always suspect they will go on to suggest I be taken from the place I happen to be and hanged by the neck until dead. I looked at Mr Drain's colleague. He was wearing a shabby grey suit and his face was the colour of sandpaper. He looked like a man who not only had indigestion himself but was capable of causing it in other people. He would have fitted in well, I thought, below stairs in Dracula's castle.

'I have with me,' he said, indicating a piece of paper attached to the clipboard, 'a High Court Summons. Unless you immediately hand over the sum of £28,000 we will be forced to serve this summons forthwith, after which you will be —'

This was not all he said. He might have gone on to tell me that I was going to be thrown in irons or towed out to a convict ship off Gravesend, but I cannot honestly say that I remember much after the words *twenty-eight thousand pounds*. It seemed – and still does seem – a staggeringly large amount of money.

When he had finished I told him, as politely as I could, that although I was perfectly willing, *en principe*, to hand him £28,000, I did not think I had that kind of money in the bank. At this his colleague from Castle Dracula, who had been staring round him with a lugubriousness that would not have disgraced the average undertaker, said, 'This is a very nice house, very nice indeed.' He said this in the tones of a man preparing to take vacant possession of the whole place.

'It is!' said my wife brightly. 'It's a lovely house!' She went on, with a calmness I admired but could not emulate, to offer both men a cup of coffee. There was a Blitz spirit of cheerfulness about the way she did this. They said they would not drink anything. They seemed to think this might compromise them. Dracula moved his face closer to mine.

'That's a nice car outside,' he said in menacing tones, indicating a black BMW. 'Is it yours, by any chance?'

I told him it wasn't; it belonged to my next door neighbour

I told him. Mine was the old Volvo on the other side of the road. I tried not to sound offensive about this. He was clearly a man it was advisable not to offend.

Before he had the chance to tell me I had a nice CD player or a nice sofa or a nice desk or nice trousers, I said, 'I think I'd better phone my accountant.'

Mr Drain bristled visibly. 'It is useless to phone your accountant!' he said, in a slightly hysterical tone of voice. 'I have with me a High Court Summons in respect of £28,000 which —'

At the second mention of that particular sum I was already out of the room and skipping up the stairs towards my office. It seemed – as I think I have said – a very large sum of money.

My accountant was out. He often is. Or they often tell me he's out. Maybe he is hiding under his desk with a tea cosy on his head while people who owe £28,000 ring him up and scream abuse at the Dutchman who always answers his telephone.

Screaming, I am afraid, is what I was doing. I could hear my voice rising in the quiet suburban morning as I told the Dutchman there were two men in my front hall who seemed intent on confiscating everything in my house up to and possibly including my wife and children. I asked him whether this sort of thing happened regularly to the firm's clients. I went on to wonder, with heavy irony, whether this was a service they only offered to writers.

'Perhaps you thought,' I screeched at him, 'that this might be good material?'

But before I had a chance to continue this line of attack the Dutchman cut in with one of those remarks with which experts traditionally confuse the layman. 'Are they', he said, 'from Colindale?'

Even at the time I remember finding this something of a masterstroke.

I recall once having a car that was always going wrong. It was a Citroën. You would take it to have a new clutch put in or a crankshaft reassembled and then, four or five hundred pounds poorer, you would drive it away from the garage in the grip of the delusion that something that has just received mechanical attention is less likely to go wrong than something that has not. It nearly always did go wrong – usually about half a mile or so from the garage where it had just been repaired. You would head for the nearest phone box and howl curses at the garage. But the men from Citroën never faltered.[1] They never showed any emotion apart from a kind of sorrowful pity as they came back with, 'What seems to be the trouble?' or, 'From where exactly are you phoning, Mr Williams?'

They had been taught, at some management centre deep in the French countryside, that *nothing defuses anger as quickly as an unexpected question*. It didn't really matter what they asked you. They had been told to *keep calm and put the ball right back on the 'customer's' side of the net, where it belongs. Don't answer their questions until they have answered yours*. But I don't think any of them ever came up with something as classical, as beautifully simple as 'Are they from Colindale?' I thought, as I stood there, gazing down at my suburban street, that this was such a brilliantly enigmatic question it would probably cover almost any emergency, far beyond taxes or mechanical breakdowns.

I had not had the foresight to answer that as far as I was concerned they could be from Mars before Mr Drain put his red shirt round the door of my office. Presumably his friend from Castle Dracula was downstairs pricing the cutlery. Before he had got all his body into the room I hit him with the hundred-thousand-dollar question.

'Are you from Colindale?'

This was obviously the tack I should have taken earlier, instead of babbling about my bank balance. It definitely threw him. He took half a pace backwards and said he wasn't from Colindale. Already he was beginning to sound defensive. He looked as if he thought he probably should have been from

1 The owners of Volvos will be familiar with a similar technique used by those who have sold them these vehicles. I refer, of course, to 'Lifetime Care'. This does not mean that if anything goes wrong with the car during the rest of its (and indeed your) natural life it will be attended to free of charge.

Colindale. I held out the phone to him.

'You'd better talk to my accountant,' I said, 'and sort out this whole Colindale business.'

He tried to tell me once again that it was useless to talk to my accountant, but his heart was no longer in it. I could see he wanted to get to the bottom of this Colindale business. Slowly he came up to the receiver and held it, nervously, a little way from his right ear. I heard a high-pitched Dutch voice squeaking at him in full flood. His shoulders drooped. He was a beaten man.

It turned out, in the end, that I had already promised to pay £28,000 in pitifully small instalments, to the Inland Revenue at Colindale. When, over the next twelve months, I talked to my friends, a number of them seemed to think that owing nearly thirty thousand pounds was nothing. Some of them said they owed much more than that. Several spoke of a playwright who owed £700,000 and was still drinking champagne in large quantities. Some said they never paid tax on principle. Others told me I shouldn't even have spoken to the men from the Inland Revenue but fired on them, from an upper window. They were particularly horrified to hear my wife had offered them coffee. Letting them over the threshold was one thing, they said. If they broke their fast on your property you were theirs for life. Most agreed that, since Britain owed billions of pounds anyway, it was pointless to get upset over a trifle like £28,000. However, I must confess that I do not like owing money. Or rather: I don't mind owing it but the thought of paying it back does rather stick in my throat.

In the weeks after the Inland Revenue came to call I was not my normal cheerful self. Every time the front doorbell rang I whimpered and hid behind the sofa. I approached the morning mail with the enthusiasm of a man negotiating an electrified fence. I gave a low moan every time someone turned on an electric light. In the evenings – my wife said – I would sit for long periods staring at the children with hollow eyes, occasionally muttering, in a low tone, '£28,000!'

My wife said I needed a holiday.

The trouble is, I don't like holidays. They are, in my

experience, a great deal more stressful than work. At least at work you are not expected to enjoy yourself. For the holidaymaker, pleasure is compulsory. Have you ever seen the holidaymakers, decked out in cagoules, staring desperately into the windows of shops in, say, Falmouth, on a rainy day in August? It doesn't matter what the shop is *selling* – lingerie, toasters, even, perhaps, advertisements for other, better holidays than the one the poor mites are undergoing – it doesn't really *matter* whether they look at a shop or a beach or a lamp post. The important fact is that these people have been sentenced to fourteen days' hard leisure, and their concentration on each minute detail of daily existence is the sort of thing not often seen outside Alcatraz. The questions that have dogged philosophers for centuries – '*Why am I here? What does it all mean?*' – have never, for me, acquired as much urgency as when sitting in a rented villa in the South of France for two weeks, listening to people say things like, 'There are some interesting caves at Poissy Les Trois Evêques.'

Somehow, existential doubt is helped, not hindered, by the presence of a swimming pool.

My eldest son said I needed an adventure. I said I didn't like adventures; you never know what is going to happen on them. A friend of mine's father, who was in the SAS during the second world war, was telephoned by his old regiment recently and asked if he would like to go on a refresher course. He said he would. He was summoned to an expensive country house and taken upstairs to a large, beautifully furnished room on the third floor. A flunkey showed him a comfortable chair then quietly withdrew, closing the door as he went. 'That', he told me, 'was the refresher course.'

I said I didn't think it sounded very taxing.

'Ah,' said the old boy, his eyes twinkling, 'but they'd locked all the doors and windows, you see. They didn't let me out for three days.'

He seemed delighted with this. But for me routine is the essence of pleasure. Doing exactly the same thing each day at least gives me the illusion that I am going to be allowed to continue to do it.

'Go to Centre Parks,' said my youngest son. 'You can play tennis all day.'

I told him I did not want to play tennis all day. Or to live in a hut in the middle of some carefully landscaped compound and be forced to bicycle to a gigantic swimming pool with all the other families on holiday. He told me I was a miserable bastard. I told him that he would be a miserable bastard if he owed the Inland Revenue £28,000. My wife told me to stop going on about the £28,000. I said I couldn't stop going on about it. I was the one being eaten alive by the consciousness of it, I said. I was the person who was going to have to pay it. It loomed as large, for me, as did Alsace–Lorraine for the average Frenchman in the early 1870s.

'Shoot yourself,' said my eldest son. 'That usually works.'

I said if someone didn't make a helpful suggestion soon that was what I would do. They would all be sorry then, I said. They could pay the mortgage and deal with the VAT man and the Inland bloody Revenue and the —

It was at this point that my middle son looked up and said, in a dreamy voice, 'You should go on the river.'

We all looked at him open-mouthed. He doesn't say much but when he does speak it's usually worth listening to him.

'You should go up the Thames,' he went on, 'in a boat. Take a couple of friends. That would be ideal for you. You'd be away from it all but not *too* far away from it. Weather's nice too.'

Then he smiled in an openly satirical manner. 'You could take the dog too,' he said, 'like in *Three Men in a Boat.*'

He lay on his back on the floor and started to cackle madly. He made cycling movements in the air with his legs.

'You could write a book about it,' he went on in a strange, high-pitched voice, 'like Jerome K Jerome. You might even make some money. Think of that, oh mein Papa!² You might

2  The word he actually used when addressing me was not 'Oh mein Papa' but 'Frogspawn'. He frequently addresses me by this name, ever since I was described as 'Nigel Frogspawn' by the English satirical magazine *Private Eye.* I did not use this in the context principally because it sounds unbearably twee. Family endearments, however, have a habit of surfacing in public in just such an embarrassing way. They create a

even make £28,000.' Then he rolled over on his stomach and cupped his chin in his right palm. His blond hair fell across his face as he said, gazing with sudden seriousness into my face, 'it wouldn't be the same, you see. Or rather it would be the same, but it would be totally different. *You can't step into the same river twice.*'[3]

That, in all truth, is how I came to go on the river. And how I came to be writing this book, following in the footsteps of a man who has been dead for over fifty years – actor turned penny-a-line journalist, magazine owner, playwright, friend of H G Wells and author of one of the greatest pieces of comic writing in English, the man *Punch* called 'Arry K 'Arry. Jerome Klapka Jerome.

weird effect at such moments, very like that engendered by people who have put on paper hats for Christmas lunch and then forgotten they were wearing them. The most embarrassing private endearment I ever heard used in public was by a woman in Finchley, who addressed her husband, in the lounge bar of the Swan and Pyramids, as 'Monkey Dear Mine' while asking him to get her a large gin and tonic.

3   One of the few surviving quoted remarks of an early Greek thinker called Heraclitus who is thought to have had an influence on emerging Greek science. The other famous remark attributed to him is 'Everything is in flux', which seems to hit the mark pretty neatly.

# Two

*Jerome's curious life – Veracity of story teller – Objections of wife to boating – Thoughts on middle age – We are introduced to Alan – His style described – Importance of secretaries in his life – JP enters the scene – We visit Kingston and become aware of difficulties with our companions.*

Jerome K Jerome was born in 1859, in Walsall, Staffordshire. His father was one of those people who started out with money but, like Trollope's father, seems to have had a God-given talent for losing it. He squandered most of the family fortune by trying to start a coal mine and Jerome, from the age of four, was brought up in East London. 'There is a haunting terror about the East End,' he wrote in his oddly secretive autobiography, and the painful, genteel poverty of his early years stayed with him for the rest of his life.[1]

Both his mother and father died when he was in his early teens. After their deaths, Jerome lived alone, working as a clerk for the Great Western Railway. It was a bleak, lonely existence and at times his account of these early years sounds like the authentic voice of one of Dickens's orphans.[2] Jerome's

1 During this period of his life Jerome was often close to total destitution. His elaborate description of the female suicide in *Three Men in a Boat* is written straight from the heart.
2 The biographical material in this section is principally derived from Joseph Connolly's biography, the only serious study of Jerome K Jerome in English, (Orbis, 1981). The only full-scale critical study of him is in German and any insight it may have into him has been denied me as

route out of the world of desperate, respectable poverty is almost pure Nicholas Nickleby. He went on the stage, and wrote a series of comic sketches about the experience called *On The Stage – And Off*, which were printed in a popular paper. From there he went on to become a well-known author and playwright.

*Three Men in a Boat*, first published in 1889 when Jerome was thirty, is the story of a trip up the Thames undertaken by Jerome, a friend from his early years in cheap lodgings called George and a third man by the name of Harris. They are accompanied by a small fox terrier called Montmorency.

Both George and Harris, as Jerome is at pains to point out in the introduction to the book, are 'creatures of flesh and blood'. George was a man called George Wingrave, who worked in a bank, while Harris's real name was Carl Hentschel. He was a character of Polish origins whose father introduced photo-etching into the United Kingdom. Jerome also emphasises that the story of these three young clerks as they row up from Kingston to Oxford in a type of boat now scarcely seen on the Thames, a double sculling skiff, is a true one.

The chief beauty of this book lies not so much in its literary style, or in the extent and usefulness of the knowledge it conveys, as in its simple truthfulness. Its pages form the record of events that really happened. All that has been done is to colour them; and for this, no extra charge has been made.

*Three Men in a Boat* is very much a boy's book and my wife did not view the idea of my trying to re-enact it with much enthusiasm. The less enthusiasm she displayed, the keener I became.

'They can't get you on the river,' I said to her. 'If the Inland Revenue call again you can tell them I am somewhere between Kingston Bridge and Pangbourne.'

German is a language in which I can only say things like, 'How far is it to Darmstadt?' and, 'I would like a cup of coffee please.' Perhaps this neglect is a by-product of what Jerome's friend the Zionist author, Israel Zangwill, called 'sneering down the humorist'. He also controlled and helped to start a monthly magazine called *The Idler*. He was much in demand as a public speaker and, until a disastrous libel case in 1898, was the editor of a popular weekly called *Today*.

She was of the opinion that they could get you anywhere. She said the Inland Revenue probably had a river division. Men in diving gear – she said – were probably even now swimming up to some barge moored below Sunbury Lock and waving waterproof High Court Summonses at the skipper and crew.

'Anyway,' she finished, 'you're a middle-aged man. You can't row. You will be run over by a steamer or something.' I take exception to being called a middle-aged man. The fact that I am 45 (fifteen years older than was Jerome when he made the trip) has nothing to do with anything. I don't *feel* middle-aged. And yet the world is constantly providing me with evidence that supports the theory that I am no longer as young as I was.

The other day, for instance, a friend of mine, who is a guitarist with a famous rock'n'roll band, was performing at Wembley Stadium. In private life he is a quiet, thoughtful individual who likes nothing better than a chat about particle physics or the latest Iris Murdoch novel. But put him on a stage with some dry ice, a few thousand kilowatt lights and the kind of speakers big enough to house a family of four and there is no holding him. He screams. He sobs. He simulates intercourse with his electric guitar. And his fans, of whom there are literally millions, stand on the seats, perform Hitler salutes and wave large, plastic bananas as if their lives depended on it.

He once offered my wife and me tickets for one of these events. When we arrived at Wembley there were several thousand people already there. Quite a lot of them seemed to be buying or selling tickets. As we got out of the car, a youth came up to us and, pointing at the tickets I was clutching to my chest, said: 'I'll give you a hundred for them.' I didn't like to say that I was a friend of the lead guitarist. The youth was looking at me in the pitying, tolerant manner reserved for those with not long left on this planet.

'Two hundred!' I must say that I was tempted. I think my face must have betrayed the fact that, in Our Price in Putney, I have been seen to look longingly towards the Easy Listening section. The youth leaned forward and leered invitingly at my wife.

'Go on,' he said. 'Go out and have a nice meal.' Although I did the right thing and went in to the concert, I think that was the day I officially entered middle age.

I began to cast about for other middle-aged men to accompany me. Most of them, of course, are not let out much, as they have wives and children, but you can still see the odd one or two in the Duke's Head by Putney Bridge, trying to behave as if they were twenty years younger. My friend Ron is rumoured to spend most of his waking hours there. I have heard it said that the management have made up a little bed for him in the back room for those occasions when he is too tired to walk the fifty or so yards home. Ron is a saxophonist. He is a short, muscular character who looks as if he would know how to behave in an open boat.

After a few hours' discussion with the local community, it became clear that it would not be a good idea to take Ron. People said that it was probably not a good idea to go round the corner with Ron, let alone row up the Thames with him. He was liable to turn violent, they said. Two weeks afloat with me would almost certainly bring him into the extremely dangerous category. Should I perhaps take Derek? Derek, I said, was an amiable bloke. My wife pointed out that I disliked Derek intensely. The last time I had been out with him, she said, I had described him as 'loathsome' and 'almost entirely ruined by therapy'.

I can never remember whom I like and whom I dislike. Derek, too, was clearly out of the question. Women are extraordinarily observant about things like this.

In the end it was obvious. I had to take Alan – if only because the last thing one could imagine Alan doing is rowing up the Thames in a skiff. Alan is a man who belongs in exclusive ski resorts and fashionable restaurants. There are those who maintain he sleeps in his Armani suit. In fact, the more I thought about taking Alan the more committed to the idea I became. I thought it would be good for him.

'Take off your Armani suit,' I said to him one night. 'Leave behind your dark glasses and your Timberland shoes! Throw off the cares of business and come and live the simple life with me on the river.' 'How long for?' he said, looking like someone who is trying to deal with an unwelcome offer of marriage.

I told him he had to stop thinking like that. I told him he was becoming obsessed with his work (he's something very important at the BBC). I told him that down on the river, the water rats were peeping out of their holes, the swans were drifting in stately fashion on the current, and the weeping willows were bowing over the water that still runs, sweetly, past Hampton Court, Windsor, Runnymede and Henley.

He gave me an odd look. 'Is someone paying you to do this?' he said. 'Because if they are, I would like a cut.'

That is typical Alan. Business, business, business. I told him that no one was paying me to do it. Who would be stupid enough to pay someone like me to row up the river with two men and a dog? Alan said there were plenty of people stupid enough to do just that. They came into his office every day, he said.

'It's unbelievable!' he went on. 'They don't even know what they're doing. They claim to be in the television business but they have no idea.' He started to bang the table. 'The other day,' he said, 'someone wanted to do a drama series about deep sea divers. Can you imagine? Glug, glug, glug! You might as well have people reading the news in gas masks, or people presenting quiz shows with bags on their heads. They have no idea!'

There was no stopping him after that. Once you have got Alan on to the subject of television it is impossible to get his mind on to anything else. Once he told us about the deep sea diving man he had to tell us about the man who wanted to make a series of programmes called Great Restaurants of the World, or the man who filmed a world exclusive interview with a lens cap fixed firmly on his camera. We ended up in an Italian restaurant, discussing things that had absolutely nothing to do with the river. I tried to bring up the subject once more when we parted.

'Ring my secretary,' he said as he staggered out into the night. 'She has the diary.'

The next day I rang his secretary. I didn't ask to speak to him. I counted myself pretty lucky to get through to his secretary. You can never speak to him. He is always in a meeting. If he isn't in a meeting he has 'somebody with him'.

'He has . . . somebody with him,' she says, cautiously, slowly, as if trying to allow you the maximum possible scope for imagining what they are getting up to in there. Sometimes she gives you a tantalising hint of the flavour of this 'meeting'. Sometimes she says it in hushed, reverent tones as if Alan were with someone so important I could not possibly begin to visualise. Sometimes she sounds quite larky about it, and I imagine him leaping about his office in a tracksuit with his personal trainer. Sometimes she says, 'I might be able to break in if you want me to.' This is her way of saying he is probably banged up with some low form of life like me or Ron.

'It's about a trip I've planned for him,' I said. There was the sound of rustling pages from the other end.

'He can't possibly do anything before November 23rd,' she said. It was then early April. I pointed out that late November was not really the ideal time to row up the river Thames.

'What's all this about rowing up the river Thames?' she said, in a suspicious tone of voice. 'I don't know anything about this.'

I explained that Alan and I were rowing up the Thames together. That we were going to hire a skiff, and moor in quiet places on the river. We would sleep in the boat, I said, under a canvas awning, as Jerome, George and Harris had done, or we would camp out under the stars.

'I can't see Alan doing that,' she said. 'Anyway, he has meetings wall to wall until November 23rd.' I asked who he was meeting, and she told me he was meeting the Head of Planning and the Assistant Head of Design and the Financial Controller of this and the Managing Director of that. He wasn't free for lunch, she said, until early in 1995. He was giving after dinner speeches, he was going away to hotels in the country 'to think'. He was more or less continuously in meetings for the foreseeable future.

The more I heard about his diary the more determined I became to get him on the boat. But I was clearly not going to get much help from his secretary.[3] The only way, it seemed, I had a chance of getting him in that skiff was by leaping down at him from a low wall as he was on his way to Television Centre, slipping a chloroformed bag over his head and driving him down to Kingston Bridge at gunpoint.

'You think you've got problems,' his girlfriend said to me. 'I only see him for about five minutes a week.'

In the end I decided to get the third man before I got the second. If I could find the right third man, he might tempt Alan into the boat. Perhaps the third member should be a young, attractive female. My wife didn't think this a very good idea. Perhaps, she said, I should get Stella Artois to sponsor the trip, or have someone film the entire proceedings. 'He might be tempted,' she said, 'if he thought it was going to be the sort of boat where things happen.' I told her that things didn't happen on boats. That was the whole purpose of going on them.

We thought about Colin and Dave and Peter and even considered, briefly, the possibility of Heinrich. But, in the end, she said, 'take JP.'[4]

Now I think back – it was at those words that the trip moved from the possible to the actual.

JP is, unlike me, a born traveller. They used to say in the Documentaries Department at the BBC that JP had a motorbike at most of the major airports of the world. He is by training an anthropologist, and has spent a large part of his adult life among distant tribes in the rainforests of the Amazon. When I rang him he was on his way to Tibet. 'I have,' he said, 'to nip up to Lhasa for a couple of weeks. But I would *love* to go up the Thames, and it would be *very* good for Alan.'

---

3  In fact Alan has three secretaries, none of whom is individually anything like as strict as the composite portrait attempted here. Taken together, however, they are quite formidable, which perhaps explains the slightly sharp tone of this passage.

4  JP stands for John Paul. People who do not know him well sometimes try and give it a Gallic flavour when they say it out loud; one man, when mentioning his name to me, gave a kind of shrug and said ' 'Ow eez Jomporl?' – as in 'Jomporl Belmondo', the French actor. This insecurity about how his name is pronounced may have led to the use of the initials.

I told him about the secretary. He said he would deal with
the secretary. He is a man used to bribing frontier guards and
flying into remote hill stations in New Guinea. The secretary,
he said, would be no problem.

I saw him three days after his phone call to Alan's office.
He was still white from the experience. 'He's booked up till
November 23rd,' he said. We decided not to count on Alan.

'We'll set about preparing for the trip,' JP said, 'and when
we meet him we'll talk about it and say what fun it's going
to be, then he'll be dying to come. He hates being left out
of things.' I thought, but didn't say, that the things he hates
to be left out of would not include sleeping in a boat with
me and JP.

'They started,' I told him, 'from Turk's Boatyard in
Kingston. Just below the bridge.'

When JP got back from Tibet – a journey that seemed
to involve far less trouble than my own modest trip up the
Thames – he and I drove down to Kingston on a cool spring
afternoon.

Turk's Boatyard, to my surprise, turned out to be still there.
And it looks almost exactly the same as it does in a guide to the
river published in 1899, ten years after Jerome's trip. JP and I
wandered in to find a young man alone at a desk littered with
papers. He was drinking a pint of bitter from a plastic glass.
He looked depressed. I started to explain that we wanted a
boat. He said they had one of those all right if that was what
I wanted. It was eighty feet long and would accommodate
nearly 250 people at a squeeze. I said I wasn't looking for that
kind of boat.

'We want to row,' I said, 'we want a double sculling skiff.
The kind of skiff you can sleep in.'

He looked at me as if I were mad. A friend of his came
in. 'He wants a rowing boat to sleep in,' said the young
man to his friend. They both examined me sympathetically. I
think they suspected I might be homeless. Eventually, a man
with a blazer and an authoritative manner arrived. Things
improved.

'Oh,' he said, after I had told him what I wanted, 'you want the three-men-in-a-boat job. Constable's of Hampton,' and he gave me their number.

It sounded from his description as if they supplied everything including the dog and a few free copies of the book. I don't know why, but I found this vaguely depressing. There is almost no kind of experience to be had these days that hasn't been pre-digested. JP, who had recently been up Everest, said every hundred yards he came across discarded cylinders of butane gas. Base camp – he said – was like a cross between an international television festival and a camping exhibition at Olympia. Even among the remote tribes of the Amazon, he said, you find the lads wearing T-shirts advertising Kronenberg lager. He reminded me of a six-foot-six native American whom he had filmed some years ago, a man whose magnificent features seemed carved out of stone. He did not seem, said JP, to belong to our century at all as he stood with his arms folded, at the edge of the reservation in the remote area of America where he and his proud tribe had been confined. JP approached him and, having a few words of Iroquois (or whatever it was the man spoke), asked him whether he would speak into the magic machine that he (JP) had brought over the sea in a bird that flies in the sky. He assured the chief that he did not seek to steal his spirit or trap him with the magic box that he carried, but would, thanks to the magic of the white man, preserve the chief's words on the history of his tribe for many moons. He said that it would be a proud day for him to hear the words of the chief and he would carry them back over the sea in the big white bird so that his people could watch a magic screen, which many of them had in their tepees, on which they were used to seeing many things, many faces, many countries of the world, and he hoped that we were all brothers under the brother sun and sister moon.

The native American looked at him oddly and then replied, in flawless English, 'How much?'

Before JP could formulate a suitably tactful response to this remark, the chief went on to say, 'Interview $50. Piece to camera $250.' Then he turned on his moccasins and strode off into the gloaming.[5]

I thought about this as we drove back to London. Perhaps I had decided to undertake a journey which was too easy, too tame, too lacking in complications to be really inspiring. Perhaps I should have gone, as JP had done the previous year, to look for the yeti, or in search of white water in the far north of Canada. There was something too easy, too domestic about the Thames.

In the end there was nothing easy about this trip. As JP said when I dropped him off at Hammersmith, 'Getting Alan on to that boat makes the north face of the Eiger look like child's play.'

5   Curiously enough a BBC cameraman, Mr David Whitson, met the same Indian in 1975 and I have other reports of his playing the same trick on Mr Mike Southen and several other film crews. For another coincidence of the same kind cf. Chapter Ten of *Three Men in a Boat* where both George's and Harris's father have precisely the same experience (bed invasion by stranger who turns out to be the friend) although in different paths at different times.

There are those who argue that such stories are 'urban folk tales' or 'old chestnuts' but those who doubt the original authenticity of the native American story should study the current, popular story in which Bob Dylan turns up at the house of a man he thinks is Dave Stewart of the Eurythmics. In fact, Dylan has landed on the doorstep of a completely different Dave Stewart, a carpenter who simply happens to live in the same area of North London. The carpenter is out and his wife asks Bob Dylan (who has not introduced himself) to wait in the kitchen. On the carpenter's return, his wife says, 'there's a man waiting for you in the kitchen. I've given him a cup of tea. I think it's Bob Dylan.' This story, while containing elements of the urban folk tale (its dialogue clearly is a later addition) was nonetheless personally authenticated for the author by a senior official at Dave Stewart's record company who described the story as 'absolutely true'. A researcher has traced the classic story of this type, in which a granny dies while on holiday abroad and is smuggled back into Britain under a tarpaulin on the roofrack – in the 1940s. But although it is always told as true, as having happened to a friend or relative of the narrators, this does not seem in my view to automatically invalidate it. The granny-on-the-roofrack story may be an expression of deep-seated British neurosis about foreign burial practices, it may, conceivably have actually happened, although in the dim and distant past. We all want to lay claim to good stories, but a story can be enjoyable or powerful *and* true.

# Three

*We begin work on Alan – His weak spot discovered – Communication on train journeys discussed – Constables boat yard is visited – Authenticity of Badger – I begin to plan our journey – Home Sweet Home.*

Over the next few months, on the rare occasions when we were dining in the presence of Alan, JP and I spent a lot of time talking about the simple joys of boating. We would put our forks to the side of the plate and I would say something along the lines of, 'Just think, down at Boulter's Lock the leaves are just coming out. Think what it would be to be camping out under the stars along that stretch from Cliveden Woods.'

Or, 'Rowing is apparently the best exercise for the executive under stress. Something about the rhythm of the *pull* as the water closes over the oars, and you breathe in the sweet air of the home counties, gives you a unique opportunity to improve cardio-vascular performance.'

Al would merely look blank. He has always been suspicious of the countryside. Some years ago we were on our way to a place in the North of Scotland. We were driving through a hillside covered with heather, looking down on a remote loch. 'Let's get out', I said 'and walk up that hill.' Alan bit his lip. 'Why?' was all he said.

I tried to get him interested in the artistic aspect of the thing. 'The success of *Three Men in a Boat*,' I would say lightly as we toyed with a little goat's cheese in a local bistro, 'depended

27

on the fact that this was one of the first books that spoke up for the newly literate mass. The small clerks who make up the heroes of H G Wells's novels described in John Carey's book *The Intellectuals and the Masses*, don't talk about "people" but about "johnnies" and who say "your label" when they mean "your name".[1] Al looked even more blank and went on talking about television.

In the late spring, however, we had something of a break-through. He said in JP's house at about twenty to twelve one night, 'Do we have to row?'

JP and I looked at each other. This was obviously a difficult question. But the fact that he was even prepared to ask it was encouraging. A lot would depend on our answers.

Alan – as a powerful executive – is, or has become, a skilled negotiator. He knows when to lower his eyes as in mourning or while waiting for someone else to raise the price. He knows when to lose his temper, strategically. He knows when to bluster and when to remain silent. We were, after all, supposed to be retracing the journey undertaken by Jerome K Jerome. Once we decided not to do it in a rowing boat, where would it all end? We could start agreeing to do the thing in a power boat and, before we knew where we were, we would find ourselves signed up for two weeks in Eilat or booked into an international conference on videograms at the Nairobi Hilton.

1  Critical response to Jerome's book was not favourable. Most contem-porary critics did not like the fact that it was written in 'colloquial clerks' English'. In fact, the critics did not start to take Jerome seriously until his work was in decline – an all too familiar pattern. The public, however, took to the book from the first. It has been translated into almost every major language of the world and has never been out of print since publication. When in 1989 I went to Prague, just after the velvet revolution, the only book translated from English I saw in the shops was a copy of *Three Men in a Boat*. It has been reprinted in various illustrated editions and filmed, but never very successfully. Although, up to now it has escaped being turned into a musical, the perfect production would probably include songs of some kind and be staged *en bateau* in Cliveden Reach. The audience would follow in steam launches while the performers (ideally including Stephen Fry and Hugh Laurie) re-enacted the trio's adventure.

'The thing is,' Al went on, 'my sister-in-law has a boat.' He said this in tones that suggested it would be the size of the *QE2*.

'They could come along too!' I said, anxious not to put him off. 'They could tow us.' And then, hardly daring to believe the progress we had made, I started talking in keen animation about some business matter or other.

It was a week or so later that JP made one of the most daring moves in our campaign. 'Don't feel,' he said to Alan, 'that business has to stop just because you're in a rowing boat. You could have meetings in the boat if you liked. If you want, we could get you a mobile phone.'

Alan's eyes brightened.

'A mobile phone,' he crooned wistfully, sounding a bit like Mr Toad catching sight of his first motorcar, 'a mobile phone!'

I can't bear mobile phones. A friend of mine saw a chap using one on the summit of Helvellyn the other day. Whenever you are sitting on a train, settling down to a couple of hours' uninterrupted reading, or looking forward to the chance of ordering a large gin and tonic at a quarter to nine in the morning, there will always be some idiot in a suit who produces a black rectangular object the size of a Jumbo Mars bar, holds it lovingly to his ear and with a slight lift of the right shoulder coyly to indicate that this is a private conversation, says things like, 'Julie, it's Kevin. Any messages for me?'

There never are any messages for him. It is always horribly clear that whoever he is talking to has absolutely nothing to say to him – probably because he rang her in the taxi on the way to the station, on the platform when he was waiting for the train and in the corridor as he and his black briefcase headed for the reserved first-class seats. Then, when he's phoned Tom in the office and Pete in Planning and a few other people, none of whom has anything whatsoever to say to him, he puts the phone away. Just as he's tucked it safely under some flow chart or other and stored it in the overhead luggage rack and is peering at some important-looking statistics, it rings. By the time he has got the briefcase down and found the phone and taken it out of the briefcase, whoever it was has given up, so he has to ring Julie or Tom in the office or Pete in Planning to see if they by any chance were trying to call him, which of course they weren't.

No one in his right mind would call him as he's probably one of the most boring creatures in the whole of the United Kingdom. But he calls a few more people just to make sure it wasn't any of *them* trying to get in touch with him and, having ended the call and tucked the phone safely away under the flow charts, he returns to his statistics. Then the machine rings again.

At this point the other passengers usually elect a spokesman and tell him that if there is any more of this he will be pushed out on to the track while the train is in motion. Then —

'What kind of mobile phone?' went on Al. 'Can I have one of those new Japanese ones?'

Before he could ask for a fax machine and a drinks cabinet JP and I said we would go down to Hampton and research the boat.

'Ask them,' said Al, 'if we can have an outboard motor, in case we get tired.'

Constable's is about a mile or so down from Hampton Court, where Harris got lost in the maze. I rang the yard and asked them whether they would be there.

'We'll probably be there,' said the man, not seeming sure about this at all.

There is a delightful vagueness about river people. They just don't run on the same time as we do. When JP and I got to the yard – it was closed. A man next door said the boatman was usually there.

'Sometimes, of course,' he added darkly, 'he isn't.'

We went down a narrow passage to the right of the boat house and came out facing about ten or fifteen skiffs, some of them decorated with green awnings stretched tightly over sets of iron hoops. They looked, I thought, like larvae about to hatch a set of smaller craft.

One or two of the skiffs were open. Most of them were not much more than a yard across at their widest and riveted with what looked like brass or copper. The prow of each one swooped up to a point as precise and threatening as the cutting edge of a Viking ship. They were about three man-lengths – eighteen feet or so from end to end.

'They're *beautiful*,' said JP in a whisper.

They were too.

There was no one around. JP stepped out on to the nearest skiff and started to examine it. There was a large, comfortable-looking chair astern and two lines back to the rudder. In the centre of the boat were two planks for the oarsmen.

'One person,' said JP, 'sits on this kind of *throne* and steers while the two others sit facing him like galley slaves and scull away like crazy.'

We looked at each other. I think we both knew who would be sitting on the throne and steering. I spoke for both of us when I said out loud, 'He can bloody well row as well!'

JP smiled slightly. 'Once we have got him on the boat,' he said, with just a hint of a German accent, 'he will obey all our commands.'

There was still no sign of the boatman. This, JP pointed out as we sat in a nearby pub, was perhaps as well.

'What are we going to say to him,' he said, 'when he asks us when we want to go up the river? We can't very well say, *as soon as Alan has a window in his schedule.*'

I said from what I had seen of the operation that that was probably the sort of date/time reference they were best equipped to understand. There was something magical and strange about the place. I was almost beginning to feel as if London, and all the things that went with it, my work, my family, even, dare I say it, the Inland Revenue, were acquiring a measure of unreality. As if the only world that really had a call on me was that stretch of dark water and those skiffs riding the wash of pleasure steamers in the quiet of a spring evening.

JP said we would get hold of Alan's diary and strike out a few meetings. 'I think,' he said, the German accent becoming slightly more pronounced, 'that he is ours now. The offer of the phone has enabled us to gain control over him.'

He looked back towards the river as we finished our pints.

'The only thing,' he said, 'is – where are we going to put the dog?'

Jerome, as it happens, did not actually take a real dog with him. He says in the introduction that 'George, Harris and Montmorency are not poetic ideals, but things of flesh and blood'. In fact in 1889 he was not the owner of a dog; in his autobiography he maintains that Montmorency was really based on a pet rat he kept as a child, which, even by the myth-making standards of the average fiction writer, seems a little steep.

I do have a dog. A real dog. Badger. If you want you can come to my house and meet him. Give me half a chance and I will bore you to tears on the subject of his moods, his character and his talents. Badger's principal talent, although he has some skills in the rabbit department, is for dramatic performance.

No one can look at you like Badger. He is only a small black and white lurcher, but his ability to convey a curious blend of trust and reproach would be the envy of many members of the acting profession. He comes up to you, puts his head on your knee, and as he looks up at you, his big black eyes seem to say, 'We are not here for long. I am a dog. You are a human. But for God's sake let us try and love each other. Let us be true to something before we both go to our long home in the cool earth!'

What he is actually after is a carrot. Or a piece of bread. Or a biscuit. Or anything. All he is really thinking about – all he ever thinks about – is food. But that doesn't stop him being able to use his eyes like Meryl Streep.[2]

---

2  Badger is less interested in food when you fork it out of a tin, dump it on a plastic plate and put it on the floor in front of him. He thinks this a somewhat crude approach to the business of eating. He would rather wait for a small piece of bacon given to him by a human than eat a whole can of Pedigree Chum on his own. He is, by the way, rough-coated. Lurchers are usually the result of cross-breeding – a greyhound or whippet with a border collie, deerhound or wolfhound, but Badger comes from a family of lurchers. In my view he is living proof that they should be recognised as a distinct breed.

Actually it is quite possible that every time Meryl Streep looks at her leading man and gives him the contemporary equivalent of 'Romeo, Romeo, wherefore art thou Romeo?' *she* is thinking about food. It is possible that when Sir Laurence Olivier looked down his own nose and rapped out 'To be or not to be', the haunted expression in his eyes was due to the fact that he was worrying whether someone had pinched the Twix bar he had left in his dressing room. Great performers are adept at conveying something they don't really feel and Badger is no exception.

When I got back home that evening I told Badger that he was going on the river. He was standing, staring mournfully at the pedal bin and didn't really seem to hear what I had to say. I told him that for a week or so he would be camping out under the stars with me, Al and JP. He turned, walked slowly back to the Aga and lay on the floor, closing his eyes at the pain of it all.

'He won't like it,' my wife said. 'He hates water.'

JP had told me I should make a list of everything we needed. He had to go to New York to show a film about Eskimos. I think it was Eskimos.

My wife is always making lists. When I am shaking up cushions in the drawing room, quite often a faded piece of paper flutters out and falls on to the carpet. On it may be written:

> Butter
> Soap dish?
> Brown bread
> Yoghurt
> Batteries
> Olive oil
> Ring Penny re Sardinia
> Macaroni for week-end if time

Like Virginia Woolf, she believes that one gains a certain control over macaroni by simply writing the word down.

I didn't think that any list I could devise would be quite up to her standard. I tried to hint, subtly, that she might like to do a

little list for me. She was brusque about this suggestion. She
muttered things about having a full-time job, three children
to look after and most of the domestic arrangements of our
house to supervise. She wasn't, she said, like some of these
women who just lay around all day having their legs waxed. I
asked if she would like her legs waxed. She said she could not
think of anything more boring or insulting. I asked her, if that
were the case, why was she so bitter and twisted about those
women who did? She replied, even more brusquely, that she
wasn't going to bandy words with me, and that *she* wasn't the
one who was going to row up the river with Alan, JP and a dog
who didn't want to go. I said it was all much easier for Jerome,
George and Harris. They were all looked after by someone
called Mrs Poppets. In the 1880s, I said, before the advent
of feminism when a man like Jerome could actually dedicate
a book to his pipe[3], things were ordered better. All any man
required, really, I told her, was a lady along the lines of Mrs
Hudson, the woman who looked after Sherlock Holmes. After
this the conversation became somewhat heated.

My list took about two weeks to compile. It read, finally:

> 1 bot Scotch
> 6 bots white wine
> (How keep them cold?)
> 3 bots red wine
> Pork pies

---

3   A book called *Novel Notes* re-issued by A Sutton in 1991. One of the
few works to have the same odd flashes of brilliance as *Three Men in
a Boat*, it is based on a very modern idea, presenting raw anecdotes
of the material of the novel instead of the novel itself, rather in the
manner of *Flaubert's Parrot*. I can't imagine two writers more different
than Samuel Beckett and Jerome K Jerome, and yet at times they do
share the same crazed attention to detail and a perverse delight in
not advancing the narrative. In spite of the persistently condescending
attitude of the literary establishment (one well-known writer recently
described Jerome to me as 'jocose'), Jerome's comedy, like *Diary of a
Nobody*, is more cunning than it looks. As with Wodehouse, he is often
deliberately satirising the manner he affects.

It lay accusingly on my desk the whole time JP was in New York. I carried it with me when I went out. I got it out and studied it in the back of taxis, hoping some new thought would occur to me. But, like *Kubla Khan*, it seemed to hang in the air like an unresolved chord. Pork pies had stalled it for good.

I still hadn't got beyond those pork pies when JP rang from Heathrow to say that he had got some dates out of Alan's office.

'He has two days free either side of a weekend in July,' he said. 'Book us up for a week. If his office get desperate they can always send out a helicopter.'

His voice sounded excited. 'We're on!' he said. 'I'm going to get a water purifier, and I have the tent I used on Everest.'

I didn't say anything to him but, not for the first time since I had had this ridiculous idea, I wasn't entirely sure that I wanted to carry it through. I put the phone down, walked back into our kitchen and looked out at the quiet peace of our suburban garden.

# Four

*Thoughts on outer London – Concerns of the experienced traveller – Need for and purchase of kit – The encirclement of Alan – Jerome's oeuvre – Secret of success of* Three Men in a Boat *– I start my journey.*

I have always loved the London suburbs. For me the words 'Muswell Hill' or 'Palmers Green' have an incurably romantic sound. 'Wimbledon' if pronounced with the right expressive intonation, can move me to tears. And, of all the London suburbs, the one in which I find myself living (I have never lived anywhere else but on the fringes of the capital) has always seemed the nearest to perfection.

This could be why, if I have to go away on business, even for a weekend, I behave as if I were about to start a twenty-year stretch in Long Kesh. My family respond well to my impression of a man condemned to death. They hang onto my clothes at the check-in desk. They wave energetically as I head towards passport control, and I know as I strap myself into my seat and as my aircraft roars up into the clouds that somewhere up there on the roof of the departure lounge are four small faces lifted up to the sky. If Al was the Mr Toad of our trio and JP was the resourceful Ratty – there seems little doubt that I was cast as the timorous, home-loving Mole.

I started to worry about the sanitary arrangements. Where would we relieve ourselves? Would we have to moor near gentlemen's lavatories? Was there a guide which contained

37

information of this kind? If there was – would it contain information about the wrong kind of gentlemen's lavatory?

I became concerned too about how we would sleep. I could not, somehow, see myself, Alan and JP on the floor of a rowing boat. All I knew about JP's tent was that 'it had been up Everest'. It was probably the size of a carrier bag. I imagined JP and his fellow mountaineers nailing their anoraks to a wall of ice and settling down to eight hours' kip with a 30,000-foot drop waiting for them should they make an unscheduled move. All he would say about his tent was that 'you could put it together in the dark with both hands tied behind your back'. It sounded as if he fully expected us to operate under these conditions.

I decided to go to our local shop and buy another, perhaps more comfortable canvas dwelling.

'I want a tent,' I said to the man, 'that an idiot could put up.'

'Do you,' he said, 'have any particular idiot in mind?'

'Yes,' I said. 'Me.'

He looked me up and down, asked a few personal questions and then as far as I could judge from the general tenor of his remarks set about dissuading me either from buying anything from his shop or even contemplating starting out on a camping expedition. He seemed to think I was more the hotel type.

The more doubtful about my purchases he got the more I bought. After I had acquired the tent I saw, above him, hundreds of attractive little packets of things designed to make the camper's life easier. There were little stoves and impacted sequences of cutlery, emergency flares and compasses, waterproof torches and a sort of tinfoil bag that, when all else failed, you could pull over your head until Mountain Rescue arrived. I bought a kind of mobile blanket bath, six months' supply of water-purifying tablets, two lilos, a bowie knife and an interlocking set of saucepans. I bought a torch, a hanging lantern, two pairs of mountain boots and a rucksack. I still don't know why I bought the rucksack. I think I thought it would help me look the part. I wore it around the house a couple of times, sneering at myself in the mirror and saying things like 'the weather's bad on Esk Pike

Traverse.' Then I put it, and the rest of the stuff, in a neat line at the end of our bed so I could look at it before going to sleep.

Camping shops are there as a sort of counselling service for anyone stupid enough to contemplate sleeping under canvas. They are also there to stiffen the nerves of the undecided. After you have spent several hundred pounds in one of them, you simply have to go.

JP had managed to tie Alan down to a date in early July. 'He's got nothing really important on,' he told me. 'He's trying to wriggle out of it, but we're holding him to it.'

I knew Alan was desperate when he said to me some time in June, 'I may have to be in Montreux.' When really cornered, he always resorted to vague appointments in the future, usually abroad. After a couple of hours of close questioning from JP, it turned out he wasn't going to Montreux at all; he was having lunch with a millionaire somewhere in the country. JP told him that it was time to stop gadding around the country having lunch with millionaires. He would have a much better time with me and JP. Alan stubbornly clung to the idea that lunch with a millionaire was a worthwhile thing to do. 'I think he lives near the Thames,' he said, eyes bright. 'I think he owns quite a lot of it.'

'No one owns the Thames, Alan,' said JP sternly. 'It belongs to all of us. It's part of the heritage of every Englishman. It runs through his bones, the way it runs through the open fields between Marlow and Henley.'

Alan said he wasn't English. He was Jewish, and he was excused games. He had a note from his mother. And he added that he was a grown man, and that we weren't going to stop him having lunch with a millionaire to go on some rotten little boat.

'We'll have to make him a concession,' said JP. 'Maybe he'll have to join us en route. I'll find out where the millionaire lives.'

The millionaire lived, not on the Thames, but on, or near, or at least in the same county as the Kennet and Avon canal. He was, apparently, a very important millionaire. It would not be

easy, JP said, to get him out of such a man's house. We would
need to find a spot on the Thames quite near to where the
millionaire lived. While Alan was in San Francisco, JP called
a conference with Alan's girlfriend, Philippa, at a pub near his
house. He got out the map and a few important looking things
like protractor, pencil and rulers and said, his brows wrinkled
in thought, 'Can you get him to Marlow?'

'I can try,' said his girlfriend. 'But you know what he's like.'
JP shut the atlas with a bang.

'Get him to Marlow Lock,' he said, 'and we'll take him on
from there.' He got that stern look about him again. 'Make
sure he has the mobile phone,' he went on. 'And a few other
things to help tempt him out. He'll need some clothes too. It
gets cold on the river at night.'

Philippa wrote all this down, then looked at me. 'He likes
fruit,' she said. 'Hard fruit.'

'Right,' I said. I wrote down hard fruit in my notebook. He
was beginning to sound like a bat.

'Unripe peaches,' she said, 'and mangoes.'

'Why don't we just let the little bastard swing in Harrods'
fruit hall for a couple of weeks,' said JP, his voice sounding
slightly strained. 'This is the *river*. He's not going to be in some
conference room with flunkies at his beck and call.'

I couldn't help thinking that, instead of flunkies, he had
got us. But then Alan has always had a way of getting people
around him to turn themselves into a sort of standing committee on his life. He is like those characters in twentieth-century
plays who are discussed, endlessly, before their appearance.
But, unlike Godot or Leftie, Alan does then actually turn
up and we all continue talking about him. He never seems
disturbed about this. In fact, he joins in the conversation
enthusiastically.

'He's had too many profiles written about him,' JP said, as
we headed back across London. 'He's had his picture in the
paper just once too often. We're going to have to be very strict.'

I booked the boat, bought a sleeping bag and, trying not
to think about whether JP's plan would work, spent the few
weeks before we set out reading up on Jerome.

I was surprised how much the man had written. There was the disastrous sequel to *Three Men in a Boat, Three Men on the Bummel* (same jokes, not as funny); the weird *Notes for a Novel* that, apart from a brilliant sequence about a man trying to light a fire, left this reader cold; an autobiographical novel, *Paul Kelver*,[1] and an unspeakable piece of whimsy called *The Passing of the Third Floor Back*, a short story which he turned into a highly successful play in London and New York.[2] He had written short stories, a not unpleasing travel book, *Diary of a Pilgrimage*, and after years of hard graft had ended his days as a pillar of the English literary establishment. His aim in life, as far as I could make out, was to be taken seriously. There were very few jokes in most of his works, and rather a lot of religiosity of a drab and earnest kind.[3]

I leafed through the only contemporary biography of him which reads more like a testimonial than a serious study. It was written in 1928, just after his death, by a family friend. The most revealing thing found in it was a picture of his wife. She looked, I thought, like Mata Hari shortly before going operational on some likely male.[4] She was wearing what seemed

1  The best introduction to 'the other Jerome K Jerome' is a book entitled precisely that. An edited selection from his autobiography, *On Stage – And Off*, and *The Passing of the Third Floor Back* and other works, it was edited by Martin Green and published by Hutchinson in 1984.

2  One of those pieces in which a Mysterious Stranger pitches up at a lodging house and gives enigmatic advice to its troubled inhabitants before departing for somewhere that is either another galaxy, heaven or a combination of the two. A bit like Priestley's *An Inspector Calls* with all of the good bits taken out, it ran for a long time in London and New York, and was even successfully revived during Jerome's life.

3  Jerome's religiosity came from his parents. His father's real ambition in life was to be a preacher in Staffordshire where, curiously enough, my own grandfather was a vicar in the early years of the century. Although it may not have done anything for his writing, Jerome was a sincere and compassionate Christian. One of the bravest things he ever did was to enlist in the Ambulance Service in the First World War. He was over fifty at the time and the experience undoubtedly contributed to his death, in the twenties.

4  This is perhaps unfair to Jerome's wife, Georgina Stanley, who has never done me any harm, apart from refusing to emerge from the obscurity in which Jerome obviously intended her to remain. All we know about

to be a length of curtain material, a massive rope of pearls and, perched on her coiffure, what might well have been a bargain basement tiara. She hardly gets a mention in Jerome's autobiographical writing. In fact Jerome comes across as the sort of man who would knock you down if you so much as mentioned his wife in public.

As George Wingrave said of him after his death, 'He never got into bed at night without saying his prayers, and I never heard him say a base word or utter any unclean thing.' The more I read about him, the more I got the impression that had he and I met he might well have knocked me down without even waiting for me to say something improper about his wife. He was as completely Victorian in his morality as was Dickens, and the kind of frankness in which modern writers specialise would have struck him as both base and unclean.

So, how did he manage to write one of the funniest books in the English language? It was, like so many good pieces of writing, a commissioned piece. He was asked by an editor for some words on the Thames – history mixed up with what was known at the time as 'humorous relief'. The editor slung out most of the history and kept the humorous relief. What was fairly clear was that Jerome had not set out to write a comic work at all.

'I did not think I was a humorist. I never have been sure of it.'

Perhaps that was the key. Perhaps the great set pieces of *Three Men in a Boat* – the forgetting of the tin-opener, or the waiting for the kettle to boil – are only funny because in a few minutes you know Jerome is going to clobber you with a few thousand badly chosen words about the historical background of Runnymede or the fact that there is an interesting church three miles south west of Maidenhead.

Perhaps. And yet . . . the conclusion I would make is that the secret of Jerome's comedy is its uniquely modern blend of truthful anecdote and fantasy. At the heart of the book

---

her is that she had one child from a previous marriage, that Jerome and she produced one of their own (who had no issue), and that, as far as we can tell, the marriage was a happy one.

is an honest desire to set down things as they actually *are*, complicated by the Dickensian urge to make the world a place redeemed by a kind word or a virtuous action. But because Jerome, unlike Dickens, was not fully in control of his material the result is pure comedy. Perhaps comedy is an accident, a bastard form, a half truth.

I thought about this on the day we set out. It was one of the few cloudless days of the summer, three or four days before the Wimbledon final and the Henley regatta – almost exactly the time Jerome and his friends had struggled down to Waterloo station about a hundred years ago. If I were a serious writer (and half of me is or wants to be) I would try to find a way of putting down that day – the blue sky behind the house tops or the chestnut trees up on the Common thrashing in the July wind.

But I find myself drawn to telling you how I wound up in Marks & Spencer in Putney High Street cramming my trolley with chicken tikka sausages, aware that, in the time it had taken JP to fly out to and return from Brazil, edit a film about Tibet and make three return trips to New York, all I seemed to have done was to resolve and fail to buy six pork pies and a load of camping equipment that no one in their right minds would want to use.

In a desperate attempt to show willing, I bought three flans, a can of chicken curry, two ciabatta loaves, three packets of pre-washed Italian style salad, four plastic tubs of bean salad in vinaigrette, a packet of prosciutto crudo and ten or twelve boxes of ready to serve meals. We would be able – assuming JP had remembered the stove – to sit down to imam bayeldi, seafood lasagna, paella valenciana and/or meat balls in spicy tomato sauce, possibly on the same evening.

I lugged all this stuff up to the house, piled it in the front hall alongside the camping equipment and settled down to wait for the sound of JP's motorbike. The last thing my wife said before she departed to pick the children up from school was, 'Watch out for vandals.'

I had forgotten about the vandals. There were bound to be vandals. Suppose they crept under the awning and on to the

boat as JP and I slept. I had a vision of myself, wrapped in my
sleeping bag like a butterfly in its chrysalis, awakening to the
sound of some Thames Valley lout with a knife between his
teeth, munching his way through my imam bayeldi.

I didn't really recover my composure until I heard the roar
of an engine outside. I whistled to Badger, ran to the door and,
to my relief, saw JP climbing off his bike. The very sight of
the man inspired me with confidence. He got 20,000 feet up
Everest. He should be able to get us to Pangbourne.

# Five

*We head for the river – Difficulties of luggage distribution – Life and times of mini-cab drivers – We meet our boat and I am introduced to the art of sculling – An interesting encounter below Sunbury Lock – Thoughts on the English class system.*

JP didn't seem as sure about this as I was. Especially when he saw my luggage.

'We're going up the river,' he said, 'not opening a car boot sale.'

He went through my equipment, throwing bits of it over his left shoulder and muttering to himself. When he had got my kit down to manageable proportions he turned with some solemnity to Badger.

'Greetings!' he said.

JP takes animals seriously. Even when eating them he seems to grasp their essential dignity. Perhaps it's all the time he's spent up the Amazon with the Wauru people of the rainforests – shy, reclusive creatures who have only ever been seen by JP and the few million people who have watched his programmes about them on television.

I asked him once how he spent his days when he was out in the jungle filming these people.

'Oh,' he said, 'you just lie in your hammock all day and get stoned. Then in the evening you go out and club a tapir or something.'

The life of a hunter-gatherer is not, perhaps, so very

different from that of a Thames Valley vandal.

When he had got us both organised, he called a mini-cab. The mini-cab driver, like nearly all other mini-cab drivers, wasn't really a mini-cab driver. I don't think I have ever actually met a full-time career mini-cab driver. They are all redundant aero-engineers or former concert pianists. After five minutes' chat with them I usually end up feeling that the economy of Britain would be much better if *I* were driving *them*.[1] 'Where-a you go?' (I think he was Turkish) he said. He looked at me, JP, the luggage and the dog. 'Your-a wives a-throw you out?'

We said that our wives had let us go away for a week or so on the river. He seemed to find this amusing. Badger sat up on his hind quarters and looked with keen interest at him from the back seat of the car.

'A man got to go out and do his thing,' he said. 'I done my thing all my life. I done it my way.'

This, it turned out, was a tactful way of saying that he had gone bankrupt, his wife had left him and he was in the process of being evicted from his flat. This sort of thing is always happening to mini-cab drivers. You never seem to get one who wants to tell you what a full life he has, driving around a battered Sierra and trying to get through to Control on the intercom. The other thing about them is, after they have told you how their house has just burnt down, how several of their close relatives have recently been struck down with fatal diseases or how they're only in Britain because they have been condemned to death for political crimes in some Middle Eastern principality, they cheer up considerably.

'Nice-a to talk to you!' he said as JP and I staggered out of

1  Once picked up, the habit of mini-cab driving is very hard to shake off. I was once taken from Hammersmith to Putney by a man who claimed to be manager and principal player of a highly successful early music group in the Netherlands. I still could not understand after questioning him for some time how he managed to find the time to drive people around London or indeed why it was necessary. He said as he turned down my offer to write a profile of him for a major national newspaper that it was a question of 'keeping his hand in'.

his car and arranged our possessions on the forecourt in front of Constable's boat yard, Hampton.

Badger went up to the nearest drainpipe, raised his off-side rear leg and with the air of quiet concentration that only lurchers can achieve began to pee. JP gathered up his gear, all neatly packaged into two bags, and I followed behind laden with about six differently sized plastic carrier bags.

The boat Constable's had chosen for us was (JP said) among his top three skiffs. It was decorated with Chinese hieroglyphs and, so a man about ninety or so years old later told me near Sonning, it could almost have been the same boat that Jerome, Hentschel and Wingrave set out in all those years ago. The rowlocks were wooden and part of the fabric of the craft. The oars, the forward pair (the bow oars) and the aft pair (the stroke oars) were both painted red for the port side and green for the starboard side.

It is wrong, really, to call them oars. 'Sculls' is the proper word. They were beautifully shaped pieces of wood twelve or thirteen feet in length, with the blades curved out in a kind of sensuous way that made you want to use all sorts of ideologically incorrect language about both craft and means of propulsion. 'She's a beauty,' I thought. 'Each scull's a stunner.' 'Sexy little number, I'd say!' also came to my mind as JP and I footed our way across the ranks of moored skiffs out to where lay our home for the next ten days.

I was mainly worried about the imam bayeldi. I was getting pretty obsessed with the imam bayeldi. Would we eat it for tea or dinner? Would it be best hot or cold? Would JP like it? Clearly in the short-term Odd Couple relationship on which JP and I seemed to be embarked I was Jack Lemmon and he was Walter Matthau. He looked pretty Walter Matthau-ish as he asked the boat man seriously intelligent questions about the rudder, the awning and the exact nature of the current. I arranged the food in the part of the boat I was going to have to get used to calling the stern. Badger had to be dragged on by his lead. He curled up between my legs and started to try to eat his tail.

JP settled himself in the control chair, seized both rudder lines and said, in his German accent, 'Villiams! You vill row!'

The boatman seemed to find this amusing. I got on to the seat, grasped an oar in each hand and, with the kind of mournful sincerity persons of quality employ to the chap designated to chop off their heads, I said to the boatman, 'Any . . . er . . . advice?'

He paused, as his trainers hovered over the stern of the boat.

'What do you mean, advice?'

'About . . . rowing and so on?'

He looked at me oddly. 'Have you rowed much?'

'Not really.' I said.

For a moment I thought he was going to order us ashore and subject me to some form of competitive examination. Then he said, wearily, 'You'll pick it up.'[2]

He gave us a brief kick and the boat sailed out in the current. JP seemed quite at home in the steering seat. He was wearing a blue baseball cap, a loose white T-shirt and black tracksuit trousers. As I pulled inexpertly on the oars, I tried to remember what came after Hampton. Was it Staines, or was it Richmond? A river subverts your sense of geography as well as your sense of time. As it loops, crazily, around the floor of its chosen valley, you come across places you thought you ought to have gone to half an hour ago and leave behind small towns you were convinced were further west (or east or south or north). There is no compass on the river. Its only logic is the constant current and the endless succession of slow curves that, finally, after long hours of labour at the sculls, add up to a journey.

2   A friend from East Molesey, Mr Warwick Gee, whose ambition is to row all the rivers in England, advised me before I set out on the journey to 'test out the old biceps'. He also suggested that I toughen my hands, adding that 'some people dip them in white spirit', to which Alan added 'and then set light to them, I suppose.' He himself, he said, used a pair of old gardening gloves while rowing, and offered to lend me the pair that had taken him up the Wey navigation. I ended up by compromising and buying a pair of brightly coloured cycling gloves.

'This is the life!' said JP, looking around him. He was already looking distinctly nautical. I wasn't sure that it was the life. Although I was able to get each scull into the water, I wasn't always managing to get them in at the same time, and when they were in the water they weren't always at the right angle to it. Sometimes they seemed to be face down, sometimes they sliced through the river horizontally. Sometimes they missed the surface altogether, causing me to lurch backwards violently.

'It's all training,' said JP. From his breast pocket he took one of the cigars he brought back from his last South American trip. Even when I did get both sculls into the current at the correct vertical plane, and not only that but managed to yank both of them back towards me with a satisfying liquid crunch; even when I managed the extraordinary feat of getting them out of the water back to their starting position and then (wonder of wonders) actually going through *the whole thing over again in exactly the same sequence* – we didn't seem to be moving. We seemed, if anything, to be going backwards.

'The current', said JP, as he blew smoke out into the evening air, 'is quite strong.' He chewed his lower lip. He sounded, now, more Devonian than German. 'She's running high,' he added fruitily. 'Yarely, yarely.'

I gave him a narrow look and threw my entire body weight behind both sculls and with the precision of a well-oiled machine repeated the sculling routine about seven or eight times. Untidy clumps of grass on the river bank inched slowly past us. About six feet above my head an elderly man on a Zimmer frame staggered towards Sunbury. He seemed, as far as I could tell, to be gaining on us.

Jerome had got to Oxford, stayed two or three days and returned to Pangbourne in under two weeks: as everyone knows, he, George and Harris had abandoned their holiday early. We'd be lucky if we got as far as Chertsey at this rate. Perhaps we should do as his secretary had suggested, and agree to meet him at Marlow some time around November 23rd. Perhaps, I decided as the sweat broke out on my brow, the thing to do was jump ship now.

'You've paid to leave it,' my father used to say, when I was unable to finish a meal in a restaurant. Perhaps we could moor the boat and check into a hotel for a few days; no one need know. Provided we stayed in most of the time or only went out in dark glasses, we would be fairly safe in Staines or Weybridge. Even if we did happen to run across someone we knew they would probably never guess that we were incapable of rowing even beyond Weybridge. There were some nice hotels in Weybridge.

While thinking all this I realised we had started to move forwards slightly faster. JP, between puffs on his cigar, was studying a book that was going to become very important to both of us: *Nicholson's Guide to the Thames*.

'You're pulling well,' he said, 'we're coming up to Sunbury!' He looked over my left shoulder. Ahead of us the river divided into two channels – which to take? 'A-starboard we go!' he said. A couple of youths who were fishing off a jetty started to shout at us. I looked away, looked down and pulled hard on the sculls.

'Pay no attention to them,' said JP. 'They're delinquent.'

It was not until we came level with them that I heard what they were saying. 'That's the wrong way, mate!' one of them was yelling, an oafish grin on his face.

JP narrowed his eyes. 'Spoils things on the river, doesn't it?' he said as I took us over to starboard.

'It's a dead end down there!' called the other boisterously. 'The lock's on the left, sunshine!'

We agreed that it was a little pathetic to see the youths of Thames Valley trying to pull tired old chestnuts like this one on people who had seen a bit more of the world than they'd bargained for. Apparently, JP said, in the Amazon basin the natives were often trying to pull off practical jokes along precisely these lines.

'Sometimes,' he said as I leaned on to the sculls, 'they will tell an anthropologist anything. That the world was created out of parrot shit or that we're all living on the back of a giant iguana, whereas their belief systems are incredibly sophisticated.'

The youths were still yelling about it being a dead end as I pulled us through quiet waters flanked by peaceful meadows. And we agreed that in a way there was something comic, almost touching, about their attempt to mislead. We could have rowed into shore and poked them on the nose for being so insolent, but the evening was so sweet, the air so calm and gentle, and this particular stretch of water so blessedly *quiet* that we were far from such thoughts.

It was, as JP pointed out after about twenty minutes' rowing, very quiet. In fact, so quiet that neither of us were as surprised as we should have been when we came to a large sign saying DEAD END. WEIR.

'It's funny, you know,' said JP, 'I could have sworn they were having us on.'

We recalled several other people, most of them seemingly respectable, none of whom had seen fit to warn us that we were rowing up a blind alley. We recalled one particular family sitting out on a plush lawn some way along the dead end who had even cheered and raised their glasses to us. One rather fat, well-dressed man waving around a bottle of what looked like rather good Sainsbury's Sauvignon, asked whether we were headed for Oxford. When we told him we were he shouted, 'Best of luck.'

We agreed as we (or rather I) rowed back the mile or so to the turn off for Sunbury Lock that well-dressed people were often the most untrustworthy.

'Give me,' said JP, 'a good honest vandal any day.'

I agreed. In fact, by the time we got back to the fork in the river, I was prepared to swear that the only really trustworthy people were liable to be illiterate, leather-jacketed thugs with more tattoos than teeth.[3]

'The real salt-of-the-earth English bloke,' I said, as we returned to the spot where the two youths had shouted at

3  There are those who maintain that the more well-dressed people are the ruder they are liable to be. Although this is sometimes true of waiters, and almost always the case for officials (the more elaborate the uniform, the nastier the person), I have not found it to be generally the case.

us, 'is probably a fairly grotty looking chap in jeans out for an evening's fishing with a few mates. He's probably the only really decent person on the river.'

I noticed as I said this, however, that both JP and I kept our eyes averted from the jetty in case the youths who had warned us were still there. I think we both felt that if they were they might both well be having a little bit of good old salt-of-the-earth English fun at our expense as we coasted across the stream back against the current, and decorously in the dying light of the July day sculled towards Sunbury Lock.

# Six

*Lock operation – I become skilled at navigation – Desborough Cut is achieved – Difficulties of communicating satisfactorily with answering machine – Importance of contacting Alan – State of public convenience at Shepperton Lock – We prepare for our first night together.*

After seven p.m. most of the locks on the Thames are self-operating. The gates were open. We moored just down stream of them and JP, who had announced his intention of rowing us up to Chertsey Mead by nightfall, jumped ashore and, when I had paddled us into the lock, closed the down stream gates, opened the up stream sluices and held our bow line as water hissed and boiled into the quiet rectangle of river.

While he was doing this I studied the Nicholson's Guide which, as far as I could see, was a fairly old one. I'm not sure how old, except that it was post-decimal and pre-all-number telephone exchanges.[1] There is, I read, a heronry

---

1 The Nicholson's Guide was taken out of the BBC library by me in 1987, when I made a film with Eric Newby called *Quickly up the Thames*. The film started with Eric on a container ship and ended up with this distinguished traveller dragging a kayak across the fields above Lechlade in search of the source. Eric has the style and grace of the kind of dandy that Jerome, Harris and George would have hoped to emulate. Those interested in reading a portrait of a real rowing man – as opposed to a hopeless wimp like me – should study Newby's picture of his father, *Something to Declare*. Newby Senior walked out of his own wedding celebration in order to have a rowing session on the Thames. After this journey, I attempted to return the Nicholson's Guide to the BBC but it seems to have slithered off to the place in which it had been hiding for

at Kempton Park protected by an agreement between gravel
diggers and naturalists, Desborough Cut was opened in 1935.
And there, shyly tucked away at the foot of page 86, I read the
important words:

> Public lavatories
> Shepperton Lock

I leafed through the guide. Shepperton Lock was about four
miles up river from Sunbury. I looked at JP as he stood by the
up river lock gate, his strong explorer's profile catching the
last of the summer sun. If he rowed as far as I intended him
to, he should get us to the nearest public lavatory just as the
dark was closing in around our little boat.

'Davidson!' I called, slipping easily and naturally into a
German accent. 'Now you will row, I think!'

JP raised his right arm and clicked his heels smartly
together. 'Jawohl, mein Führer!' he said.

I don't know why it is, but leave Englishmen of a certain age
alone for any length of time and they all end up carrying on like
Anton Diffring in *The Great Escape*. What red-blooded post-
war baby can forget Anton's cutting blue eyes as he rounds
on Steve McQueen and Richard Attenborough?

'Hauptmann Zessler vill be here in a minute. His methods
are' – short mirthless laugh – 'less pleasant than mine!'

If this carried on, by the time Alan got on board we would be
singing the Horst Wessel song in German, something my late
father actually did to an astonished group of German tourists
in the former Yugoslavia in the early 1970s.[2]

It was only when I was sitting in the wide, comfortable
steering seat that I realised that JP had been doing it all wrong.
He'd been lying back chomping on his cigar and toying with
the tiller lines in a dilettante sort of way, but actually steering
was a pretty responsible and difficult job. I said this to him as

---

   the last seven years.
2  He was prevented from finishing the song by my mother saying, 'David,
   please stop it.' My two brothers and I all argued that he was not likely
   to give the Germans any offence and that the only good reason for him
   curtailing his singing was to prevent them joining in.

he grunted over the sculls, but I don't think he took on board what I had to say.

'You've got to be ceaselessly vigilant,' I said, as I scanned the horizon for large steamers coming at more than thirty knots an hour. I tweaked the line to the left, then to the right, and skilfully brought the boat out into the stream across to the starboard bank and then back to the port side in order to keep a constant trajectory. I sought out the gentlest touches of current, steering a clear way from posts and driftwood, applying the tiller lines like Karajan conducting the Berlin Philharmonic in a Beethoven symphony.

'Why are you zig-zagging all over the river?' said JP, breathing heavily, leaning on his sculls. He seemed slightly querulous, I thought. 'Wouldn't it be easier to go in a straight line?' I smiled tolerantly. I hadn't realised that he was going to crack under the strain. Biting back the observation that the river Thames had a thing or two to teach travellers, even travellers who had spent nine months in the Gobi Desert with nothing but Magnus Magnusson and a BBC film crew for company, I played with the rudder lines easily, very much in the way I flicked the reins of my horse Dapple during my one-hour long session of pony trekking near Bath in 1979.

' Just row, my friend,' I said, a little smile playing around my lips. 'Leave the tiller to the steersman. He'll tack you yarely on the foc'sle bow and bring her under the lee shore before the easterlies blow!'

Muttering that if I insisted on yanking the rudder round as if I were trying to stimulate it sexually I would end up on a lee shore with a boat hook up my crack, JP bent once more over the sculls and drove them through the Thames with really savage aggression.

'Would you like me to cox you?' I said.

He didn't answer. I thought, perhaps, he hadn't heard me.

'I could go – *in* – out *in* – out, to help you get your stroke in the proper time,' I said.

He didn't respond to this either. I tried a few 'ins' and 'outs' as we came past Wheatley's Ait with Walton-on-Thames mercifully invisible over to my left and JP's right. But it was

hard to get him into a really good rhythm. In the end I let him
go his own way. Rowing is something you have to have in your
bones, I think.

As we came down through Desborough Cut it was beginning to get seriously dark. A boat with one red port light and
one bright green starboard signal spluttered and throbbed
towards us out of the gloom. There were small ornate villas
on either bank but no one, now, out on the quiet lawns. The
sky and the river merged as the colour leaked away from their
once brilliant faces.

'Are you ever scared when you travel?' I said to JP, with one
hand trailing in the water.

'Those single-engined planes in the Amazon are quite
frightening,' he said. 'If the engine goes down so do you. One
pilot I flew with had come down slap bang in the middle of
the jungle. It took him nearly a year to get back to civilisation.
The only way you can navigate is by the rivers. His wife was
on the point of re-marrying.'

I found the story so disturbing that I didn't dare ask what
had happened to the poor man. What I wanted to ask was
whether he was scared not by things in nature but by nature
herself. Even on the peaceful Thames, now that light and
colour were ebbing away from the landscape, I was beginning
to feel a kind of dread. Perhaps I only stay in the suburbs
because I can find quite enough to frighten me there. JP is
by no means an unimaginative person, but he is extremely
practical. He tends to be afraid only of real dangers rather than
imaginary ones.

I remembered Douglas Bader once being asked if he had
ever been seriously frightened.

'Oh,' he replied, 'I was frightened about the middle of last
week.' 'What happened?' asked the journalist, hoping for some
dark secret. 'A car pulled out of a side road a couple of hundred
yards in front of me when I was travelling about 80 mph,'
replied Bader.

I kept a keen look-out for vandals as JP pulled us in just
below Shepperton Lock and moored us at a flight of concrete
steps that led up to what I now realised was the lock-keeper's

house. I didn't, at this point in our journey, know anything about lock-keepers, or else I might not have been quite so sanguine about tying up the skiff, rolling the awning over the metal hoops and pulling out a bottle of scotch from under Badger's rear end.

Badger scampered up on to the lock and started to sniff the grass. He seemed pleased to be able to smell something a bit more savoury than camping equipment. JP was studying the Nicholson's Guide.

'We're never going to make Marlow,' he said, finally. 'You had better ring Philippa and re-schedule the pick-up point.' A couple walked slowly arm in arm up the path on the other side of the river and off towards the darkness up river of the lock.

'Where's the third man?' said the husband.

We said that he was in a meeting. I think I heard more references to Jerome from average members of the British public in the time I was on the river than ever before in my life. Some people asked if Badger was called Montmorency. Some people asked which one was George and which one was Harris. One enormous builder's labourer just outside Reading leant off his scaffolding and asked us whether we had remembered the tin-opener (we had, I think, four or five tin-openers).

But the reminder of Alan had brought out some of JP's most Ratty-like qualities. 'You'd better give him a clear idea of the new venue,' he said, 'or he'll use it as an excuse.' We agreed that we would meet him at Windsor.

'Don't talk to the machine,' called JP as he crouched over the camping gas and started to set out our equipment in neat piles just in front of the lock-keeper's front garden. 'Try and talk to him personally if possible. Make it clear there is no alternative. He must come in the boat.'

Most of my telephone conversations these days are with answering machines. When I do talk to a person I am reminded of how vague, long-winded and time-wasting they can be. Life would be much simpler if they just beeped at you and then listened to what you had to say. Machines are of course much better at listening than people.

I used to have a message recorded by my son and when my mother, who is 82, rang up she would wait for the bleep then say in a careful, polite, pre-war voice, 'Hello, Jack, it's Granny here' – rather like the old man who thought it rude not to watch television right up until the end when it closed down for the night. Some people forget that you have spoken to their machine and not to them, and ring you back vaguely aware that they should have said something to you on the last occasion when the lines were open between their house and your house but they can't quite think why they didn't. This leads to extraordinary lines such as, 'Were you talking to me or my machine?'

Don't they know? Why don't we get machines to ring up as well as take messages? Why don't we send machines out to business lunches while we head off for the river? Let the machines take over, I say, and we can all lie on our backs in the long grass looking up at the clouds moving slowly over the heavens.

As I was dialling Alan's number I decided that machines and modernity might have something to do with the extraordinary popularity of *Three Men in a Boat*. Jerome, of course, like his friend Wells, was writing about the twentieth century from the point of view of the nineteenth. Where Wells saw spacemen in the shape of Victorian engines Jerome saw the awful face of Modernity loom up over his peaceful English garden.[3]

His masterpiece is perhaps the first authentic description of a holiday in the twentieth-century sense of the word in western European literature. His three clerks aren't on an adventure or seeing the sights of Europe or really *doing* anything. They

---

3   One of the works of Jerome that has never made it out of the British Museum since publication was an essay he wrote for a collection called 'The Humours of Cycling', to which Wells also contributed. It is a heavy-handed evocation by Jerome of the young man who has 'stolen his wife's affections, and who 'walks her round the park with his arm around her waist'. He turns out to be her cycling instructor. If this is a piece of truthful autobiographical anecdote as found in *Three Men in a Boat*, it is one of the few clues we have as to how Mrs Jerome passed her leisure hours.

are simply escaping. They are three young men on a spree. Oppressed by the city and the city's demands, they seek out … well, nothingness.

It is not so easy for us. In Jerome's time there was no public call box at Shepperton Lock.

I was connected to Alan's machine. I told it to meet us at Windsor. I told it that we would be calling it later to make sure that it had told Alan just where his responsibilities lay. I told it, too, that the river was just great, and the sooner he got out of those meetings and on to it the better. Then I tied Badger up to the railings and tiptoed shyly into the gentlemen's lavatory.

It was done out tastefully in eggshell blue. It reminded me of the kitchen décor fashionable in the early fifties. Someone, apparently from the interior design department, had been hard at work on the facilities.

Perhaps this was a deliberate policy of the local council to facilitate the kind of encounters that obviously went on here. On the wall of my cubicle a man describing himself as 'in his early thirties' had suggested a meeting very different from the sort in which Alan was presumably, even now, engaged. He seemed to want to contact an unspecified number of men between the ages of 18 and 29 for something he described as 'sex fun'. In order to advertise this, on the opposite wall he had etched a tasteful line drawing of a set of male genitalia. He didn't say whether they were supposed to be his. Perhaps they were done out of pure *joie de vivre* in order to suggest the kind of things he and the other young men were going to get up to in the public lavatory at Shepperton Lock.[4]

---

4 The most touching and well-written piece of graffiti found in a public lavatory was recorded by my wife in the early 1970s. On the walls of ladies' lavatories, she tells me, the tone of the confessions is sometimes even more lurid and violent than that of the men's (or rather my account of the men's graffiti – our fieldwork has not yet extended to her entering male-only conveniences). This particular piece was written by a young man who liked to dress up in women's clothes, enter ladies' conveniences and pee sitting down in public toilets, a harmless activity, which – according to my wife – the young man described with touching lyricism. She was unable to memorise the whole thing but tells me it began, 'On Thursdays I like to wear knickers and a brassière from Janet

It was all a long way away from Jerome K Jerome. Presumably he, George and Harris would not even have stooped to read such things. Although that remark of George's, 'I never saw him get into bed at night without saying his . . .' No. Such a thing was not to be thought of.

I allowed my eye to wander further down the wall. Various other young people of the district had suggested similar meetings, and some had alarmingly specific ideas about what kind of things might take place at them. A number of the messages suggested particular times. There were even post-meeting reports. 'I was here at 9.30,' said one sad little note by my left foot. 'Where were you?'

I looked around me nervously. Had I wandered in on the equivalent of the evening surgery? Everything seemed quiet. Just in case, I started to hum in a brisk no-nonsense manner. But even this, in the present surroundings, had a come-hither quality to it. Fortunately, as far as I could tell, the favourite trysting hour seemed to be fairly early in the morning. Perhaps the Shepperton gay community liked to get it all over with before breakfast and then get down to a satisfying day at work. I stole out to Badger, unpropositioned, and he and I ambled together back over the lock to where JP was waiting.

Progress isn't all bad, I couldn't help thinking, as I came over the steps to see JP stooped over a can of soup, his pale mobile face wearing an expression I was to get to know well, even to describe to myself as camper's concentration. The high-toned morality to which Jerome, Wingrave and presumably Hentschel subscribed concealed all sorts of unhappiness. Those unable to live up to the bluff, male camaraderie obligatory in Jerome's set were forced, like E M Forster's Maurice, to rush off to the doctor and tell them they were an unspeakable of the Oscar Wilde sort.

'Soup!' said JP.

The imam bayeldi was nowhere to be found. I opened two packets of potato salad and some coronation chicken. Then I opened a bottle of wine. The two of us, our backs to the

Reger, Pretty Polly tights and a figure-hugging black dress . . .'

lock-keeper's house, devoured our evening meal. Although the view across the lock to the white power boats, muffled sleepers at their moorings, had a certain charm, neither of us took our eyes off the skiff, its awning the palest of green in the half light.

'That', said JP in tones of quiet satisfaction, 'is where we will sleep.'

# Seven

*Art of camping – Sleeping with other men – Distressing treachery of Badger – JP's sleeping habits – I am confronted by an unresolvable dilemma – Shepperton – A dramatic exit from council premises – Continued attempts to contact Alan.*

I couldn't work out why he seemed so pleased about this. It was the sort of pleasure I imagined him feeling when he looked up at a difficult chimney on K9 and turned to Chris Bonington, or whoever was roped next to him on the ice, and said, 'Just think – in a few hours we'll be up there!'

The pleasure I derive from looking at mountains is principally that of knowing that I am not on, or liable to be walking, climbing or sleeping on any part of them. The best view of a mountain is, in my opinion, from the window of a room in a nearby first-class hotel. The same goes for camp sites. From a distance they seem bright, hopeful little settlements. You look out over a valley at the blue canvas dotted around the grass of some hillside, and you can be fooled into thinking that lying down in a tent could be rather fun.[1] When you are actually in

1   It is important not to be fooled by the frame tent. In larger camping stores and some garages these things, sometimes the size of small bungalows with separate rooms and front doors, may seem attractive. 'They're like houses really,' my youngest son said, just before we bought one in the early summer of 1986. They are "not" like houses, although they take about as long to put up. And anyone who thinks that conjugal relations are possible in the canvas 'room' set aside for Mummy and Daddy in the ones they have carefully assembled in your local show room was

one and your ears and nose are inches away from the soil as a keen wind scurries through the undergrowth, it is a different story. Your right shoulder always seems to be grinding into the rockiest part of the terrain. You only discover it isn't the rockiest part of the terrain when you try to move. Perhaps your left shoulder will mould itself to the earth rather better. It doesn't. As you lie on your back and the wind whistles through the tent flap, you reflect that the only people who should be this close to nature are those who have gone through the burial ceremony.

Without my being aware of it, JP had got into the boat, abandoning our evening meal on the steps of the lock. Not only that – he had got himself inside his sleeping bag and seemed to be proposing to go off to sleep only yards away from a public thoroughfare. I wasn't looking for a bedtime story or some assistance in getting my teddy in the right place, but I had thought that I would get some measure of help in making the difficult transition from being vertical, though rather drunk, on the edge of the Thames and nestling down for what, assuming nothing disastrous happened, might well prove to be eight hours' sleep. On the other side of the lock the youths of Shepperton were driving cars and motorbikes, fast, off into the blackness. Judging by the shouts reaching me across the water, there was a party on somewhere. Possibly in the tastefully done out public convenience.

I blew up the lilo, lugged it under the awning and settled down in the stern half of the boat. Up in his half of the vessel JP had already set out his two camping mattresses with naval precision and hung a small lantern from the hoop above him. It was all rather cosy. As I was looking at it longingly, a small black and white head reared up from the bilges behind JP. Badger gave me a brief glance of wild surprise, one ear up like a sansculotte's cap, then buried his nose into the small of JP's back. He was sleeping in the captain's quarters, I thought grimly, as I worked myself into my sleeping bag.

obviously not around on a camping site near Exeter during the early August of 1990.

This is Badger, of course. He is not a dog to be relied on when the going gets rough. He doesn't think, 'This is the man who has personally opened several thousand cans of Pedigree Chum on my behalf. This is the man who has covered thousands of miles of south west London while I cock my leg up against lamp posts, trees and on one occasion the rear wheel of his neighbour's BMW.' He heads, in the manner of dogs, for higher status territory.

'Are you all right, Nige?' called JP.

'I'm fine,' I said.

If you have been married for twenty years, as I have, there is something alarming about acquiring a new sleeping partner. I must remember, I thought, as I wriggled my legs down to the bottom of the bag, not to call JP *darling* or to reach, in friendly fashion, for his left leg.

The lilo felt good. I recalled that story of Wilfred Thesiger, the great traveller, meeting Eric Newby in the Hindu Kush and remarking, on discovering that Eric and his companion were using lilos, 'My God, you must be a couple of softies.' That remark was what had prompted me to buy one. And as far as I could tell, it compared well with my mattress at home. It yielded sweetly to both shoulders. When I turned, the boat rocked slightly. Through a gap in the awning I could see a half-empty tub of potato salad perched shyly on the midnight steps. I turned over again, allowing my body to enjoy the rippling resistance of the canvas.

Then, somewhere around my rib cage, there was a quiet hissing sound.

'Can you hear that, JP?' I said.

JP yawned. He sounded, I thought, comfortable.

'Is there a snake in here or something?'

JP yawned again. 'It's probably your lilo,' he said. 'They're totally useless on a camping trip.'

Why had he waited until now to tell me this? He gave a last exquisitely modulated yawn. He sounded, I thought, like a lion after a particularly good lunch. 'The only place for a lilo *really*,' he went on, through the yawn, 'is in the swimming pool of a posh hotel.'

There was a rush of air and with a thud my right shoulder hit the wooden planks of the bottom of the boat. As it did so, JP began to snore in a way that suggested that he was not going to stop. There was something steady and contented about it.

My late father used to snore. When he really got going, the windows and doors shook. My mother moved into the spare bedroom, but that was no help. People passing on the pavement outside would cross themselves when they heard the noise coming from 110 Holden Road. My brother and I, who were in the room next door, virtually gave up the idea of sleep.

He was moved down to a room at the end of the landing. At one point it was even suggested that he be put in the garden shed, although my brother pointed out that this might well alter the ecological system of North London for ever, since no animal within a radius of 250 yards would be able to get any sleep. In the end we all learned to live with it.

I was going to have to do the same with JP. If my wife snores I reach over in the darkness, smash her in the face with my forearm and say in clipped authoritarian tones, 'Don't *snore*.' She whines a bit at first, but it seems to work. I was not going to be able to do this to JP. I couldn't see myself climbing out of a sleeping bag, crawling up to the other end of the boat and giving him a straight left to the chin in under three quarters of an hour.

After about ten minutes of this, quite suddenly, he stopped. Maybe Badger had thumped him with his tail. I emptied my mind of all provoking thoughts, breathed out slowly and prayed for sleep to come. Badger was asleep. JP was asleep. Why wasn't I?

'Because,' said a tiny irritating voice in my head, 'you are lying on the bottom of an antique wooden boat with only a deflated lilo and two inches of hard English oak between you and the Thames.' I turned over. Gradually the rhythm of the boat's hull started to jostle me towards sleep. A regular rhythm, I thought, induces sleep. That's why you rock babies. I remembered rocking our first son. I remembered leaning his head on the crook of my arm and rocking the way the boat was rocking on the river's gentle current . . . this way and that way . . . this way and way way . . . this way and . . .

My eyelids were giving a last helpless flutter and my breathing was slow and regular. I was moments away from oblivion. Then from the other end of the boat there came a noise not unlike the opening of a heavy artillery bombardment. This was followed by a whistle I have not heard the like of since a boy at school put on his father's long-playing record of steam train noises. The *snore*, if that is what it was, and not the first leg of an Iraqi invasion of the home counties, stayed with the train theme for its second appearance (not unlike track 6 on my friend's record, 'The Royal Scot on Shap Fell') then mutated to a ghastly death rattle which turned out to be JP's method of regrouping for Snore Number Three, a mélange of the first two efforts with a new effect that was not unlike someone dropping an iron bar into a still-functioning electric lawn mower.

He was presumably going to have some sort of heart attack. No one could make a noise like that, even in their sleep, and live. I could not find it in my heart to grieve for him. In fact if he didn't have a heart attack in the next five minutes I was going to get up to the other end of the boat and offer him an alternative way out of his miserable existence: massive head injuries inflicted by the blunt end of my skull perhaps, or an unanaesthetised tracheotomy with a tin-opener.

He was gearing himself up for Snore Number Four. There was a flurry of snuffles and a series of grunts that might well cause medical science to redefine the potential of the human nasal cavities. In fact, I thought, I might as well get out there, stroll into Shepperton, break into an electrical appliance shop, hot foot it back to the skiff with a cassette player and record the thing for posterity. I clearly wasn't going to get any sleep, and this was the kind of snore that had earned its right to a place in a tape library at the Royal National Ear, Nose and Throat Hospital.[2]

When he spoke I thought at first he had woken up to apologise. What he said wasn't entirely clear. It sounded, I

2 My wife maintains, although she has no evidence to support this allegation, that I snore. She even alleges that on one occasion I snored

thought, like 'Angmering'. I couldn't work out why he wanted to visit Angmering, although I felt I would approve any scheme that would enable him to go somewhere that wasn't Shepperton Lock.

I hoped that talking might interfere with the snoring. This wasn't the case. It proved to be simply part of the cabaret. In fact, I reflected, talking and snoring were probably not going to be enough for him. Soon he would be yodelling like Frank Ifield or going through all the tenor arias in *Don Giovanni*.[3]

I have read somewhere that in the shipyards of the Upper Clyde certain households next to the yard were subjected to twenty-four-hour noise from the machines on the dock as they struggled to complete an order. When the noises stopped the people in the houses found they could only get to sleep next to a recording of a few hundred welders going at it full blast.

Gradually I became acclimatised. There was something, I discovered, almost soothing about the noise coming from JP's sleeping bag. Tomorrow night I must remember to get to sleep first. If necessary I would drink myself to sleep with the evening meal and then the bastard would have to *put* me in my sleeping bag. I concentrated on the noise. Years ago, of course, our first son had often only got off to sleep when the reggae started pounding out from the house next door. The regular rhythm of the basses, throbbing out on to the street 'Kaya got to have . . .' *kaya* now in a *regular* rhythm would soothe him in the way the rhythm of the boat was . . . the rhythm of the boat was . . .

I was almost asleep when I realised that I wanted to pee.

I knew at once that this was an urge that was not going to go away. I couldn't think what had caused it. It might have been the noise of the water, slapping at the sides of the boat. Perhaps it was the fact that the boat itself was now heaving to the rhythm of JP's snores. I was going to have to go.

so violently that I woke myself up, shouted 'Stop snoring!' and lashed out at her violently.

3 People who talk in their sleep do not, whatever anyone may say, usually mutter the names of illicit lovers. They usually say things like 'there's a tortoise in my bed' or 'where's the fruit gone, Norman?'

Where, though? I couldn't face the thought of trekking back across the lock to the gentlemen's lavatory. Anyway, things were probably just warming up over there. The sight of a forty-five-year-old heterosexual man in underpants might well cast a dampener on the proceedings. I could climb out of the boat and pee on the tow-path, but somehow the journey from the bottom of the skiff to dry land seemed too long and difficult even to contemplate. Finally, I hoisted myself out of my sleeping bag down to just below crotch level and dragged myself to the starboard side. I pushed back the awning, thrust my underpants out of the way and held my equipment out through the canvas and over the side.

I don't know whether any of the lads from the gentlemen's convenience were on the opposite bank. There may well have been one or two wandering home after an exhausting night in the facility. But, if any of them allowed their eyes to wander over to the double sculling skiff moored under the lock-keeper's house, they chose to ignore what I had to offer. Perhaps there was something desperate about it. A man reduced to poking his chopper through a canvas flap and waving it across the river at three in the morning was obviously not worth bothering about.

Finally, exhausted, humiliated and seriously worried about whether there was anyone out there who had witnessed this unique violation of the bye-laws of the navigable Thames, I crawled back into the bag, pulled my head inside it as well, and to the sound of JP's throbbing snores drifted into oblivion.[4]

Those who sleep in the open are jolted into wakefulness. Suddenly I was aware of the soft green light as the early

4    The particular section of the Thames Navigation and General Bye-laws (1957) being violated here is as follows: As to offences against decency, bathing etc.
      46. No person shall while using or while in, upon or about the Thames or the banks or the tow-paths thereof or any land of the conservators:–
          (i) Commit any offence against decency or be intoxicated or otherwise behave in a disorderly manner; . . .
      I also later violated sub-section iii) of section 6 which forbids you to –
          (iii) Dress or undress except behind an efficient shelter or screen; and later Alan and JP violated section

morning sun filtered through the awning. Outside, on the river quite close to me, a duck quacked importantly. A new day! Afloat on the Thames! No phone calls! No tax man! Nothing but me and the river!

JP was still snoring. The snore seemed to have matured. It had settled down in the eight or so hours I had been asleep. The nightmarish special effects of last night were obviously early work. It was as if I had been privileged to witness the man learning to snore. This new sound was a relaxed and friendly affair, the sort of snore you could learn to like. I looked at my watch. It was six thirty. The snore seemed less attractive.

From the other end of the boat Badger gave me another wild stare of the Cortes caught silent upon a peak in Darien variety. Muttering to myself, I struggled into my T-shirt and lurched out on to the lock steps. Badger came too, and the two of us stood in the early light among the ruins of the previous night's dinner.

Now for the first time I could see Shepperton. To the west, beyond the lock, the river curved away, lined with willows and houses that, although obviously designed for habitation, were each all too obviously somebody's dream. Some were functional bungalows, others miniature wooden affairs with the folksy complexity of cuckoo clocks, and further away to my right I could see through the trees the occasional fragment of a suburban Toad Hall. Just down stream of the lock was a heron standing incognito in the shadows, waiting for fish.

I dragged Badger with me as I went back across the lock. I needed moral support to go into the gents.

For a moment I contemplated taking him in with me, but

> (iv) which states that no one shall – iv) Bathe without wearing a
>     dress or covering sufficient to prevent indecent exposure of the
>     person.
> We were all therefore exposed to the penalties set out in section 57 – a
> penalty not exceeding *£10 for every such act*. As I was probably drunk
> at the moment of urination it is possible that I laid myself open to two
> charges of £10 although if the last comes to court I will maintain that you
> cannot violate the same sub-section of the Thames Bye-Laws twice *at
> the same moment*.

then decided this might be viewed in the wrong way, were the action to be still in progress.

The place seemed deserted. I made for the central cubicle and was just about to lower my trousers when a small, perfectly groomed head appeared above the partition. He seemed pleased to see me. He had the bright, eager-to-satisfy expression I associate with the helpful gnomes of children's stories. It is entirely possible that he did not have designs on me. He might well have been a sociologist commissioned by Shepperton Council to study the habits of convenience-users at unusual hours. He could have been a member of an extreme religious sect hoping to catch a potential convert at a particularly vulnerable moment. He could, for all I know, have been a gnome straight out of a children's story. But I did not wait to find out.

Muttering (I seem to remember) 'Oh no!' I hitched up my trousers and stumbled towards the exit. Had there been any of the local vice squad concealed in the undergrowth I would, I think, have been on dodgy ground as with my trousers still at half mast, I untied Badger and headed up the right bank.[5]

I studied the Guide. Over to my right outside one of the suburban Toad Halls a large, expensive-looking car and its chauffeur waited for their early morning ride. I watched as a tubby man in his fifties, briefcase in hand, came out of the front door on his way from the green lawns, the carefully arranged villas and the lazy sweep of the river to the real world of business.

We had come about six miles last night: about one mile an hour. Assuming we started rowing in about an hour we could, if we rowed for about sixteen hours non-stop, get to within a mile of Bray. If we rowed on through the night without stop-

5  Even the entrapment of gay men in public conveniences by the police, who surely have better things to do, has its humorous side. I wrote a play on this subject in the 1970s, inspired by an interview with a member of the London vice squad who was asked what sort of clothes he wore when sallying forth to try and get other men to make advances to him. 'For this type of work,' he said, 'ordinary police clothes are obviously not suitable. We try to keep up with the latest fashions.'

ping to eat we might make Marlow by Saturday lunch when Alan was due to arrive. I made these calculations because I was not at all sure that Alan would ever get any message from us. Suppose he was in meetings twenty-four hours a day until the time came for him to be taken up to Marlow? Getting through to Alan was a bit like phoning a commercial radio station to say you've guessed the answer to the mystery quiz. It was possible that he was, inexorably, on his way to a destination we were going to be unable to reach.

How could he do this to us? I thought to myself as Badger and I wandered back to the lock. I eyed the telephone box hungrily. It was seven o'clock, not too early to call him. What right did the man have to sleep anyway? He was in a comfortable bed in West London and had probably spent last night in some sophisticated restaurant with . . . It didn't matter who with. Some smart London businessman. What did these smart London types know of life? I thought to myself as I paced up and down outside the glass box. Had they ever spent the night in a four-foot-wide skiff with one of the worst snorers in the western world? Did they face a rowing schedule that was punishing even by the standards of the average galley slave? I would call him, I decided. I would call him and give him a piece of my mind. I might well call a few smart London types as well while I was at it and give them other pieces of my mind. You may think I was being a little unfair here. I had, after all, asked the man to come on the boat. He had out of the kindness of his heart, although a very busy man, consented to come. I had no right to feel the kind of hysterical fury that was welling up inside me.

But that is what holidays do to you. You start out in sunshine with bright faces and clean luggage, looking at the scenery as if you had never seen God's good earth before. Then after a few days you are snarling at the world like a wild beast. Shaking with rage I dashed into the phone booth, dialled Alan's number and was once again greeted by his answering machine. I hung up and dragged Badger back across the lock to where the boat lay.

# Eight

JP was making breakfast. He was crouched over the camping gas and peering at it in a puzzled manner. As Badger and I came up to it he thrust his head down to the level of the ground and gave it a sidelong glance. Then, pursing his lips, he edged round it in a half circle like a sheep dog making sure that the thing wasn't going to leap up and scurry off towards the grass.

'I'm trying to see if it's on,' he said, squinting at it from the other side. 'The only way to tell if a camping gas is on is to stick your fingers in it.' For a few moments I thought he was actually going to do this. Instead he put a small kettle on top of the flame and hopped over to his rucksack. From it he took a cylindrical object about the size of a pepper mill. It had a handle to one side. He started to turn it.

'Coffee grinder,' he said. 'A sherpa on Everest had to grind this every day as his daily duty.'

I did not comment on this. Nor did I say anything as he unpeeled a pack of bacon and put three or four rashers in a frying pan. Cooking in the open air is a serious business. Cook-ing in the open air by men is a serious business, and there are as many tribal taboos associated with it in the Thames Valley as there are among the Wauru Indians. Anyone who has ever

73

been to a barbecue will testify as to the truth of this assertion.
As JP moved, rather elegantly, on his haunches along the
steps of the lock, and as Shepperton woke up around us (the
lock-keeper came out of his house with his young son, and
after a brief glance in our direction took the boy over the river,
presumably off to school), I thought about my brother John,
and his spaghetti bolognese.

'One day', he used to say to us, 'I'll make spaghetti
bolognese.'

We said that that would be nice. We enjoyed it, we told him.

'Oh,' he used to reply, 'you think you've had spaghetti
bolognese, do you?'

We said we thought we had. We said we thought there was
hardly any person in the civilised west who had not had it.
White pasta, we said, long thin white pasta, with a kind of
meat sauce. And maybe cheese. He sneered openly at this.

'I don't mean that Italian rubbish,' he said, 'I mean *my*
spaghetti bolognese.'

At this point his wife usually chipped in. 'Yes,' she used to
say, 'John's spaghetti bolognese is quite something.'

We encouraged him to get into the kitchen and start frying
right away. It sounded, delicious, we said. At this John became
rather coquettish. It was delicious, he said, unbelievably so. It
was just something he did, but anyone who had ever eaten it
said that after they had eaten it no other spaghetti bolognese
would ever pass their lips. But he wasn't going to make it
now. It took days, he said. He had to be in the mood. Things
had to be marinaded. You had to go to market, usually very
early in the morning. You needed, too, special equipment not
usually found in this country. One day, he went on, he would
make it for us. And then we would really know what spaghetti
bolognese was.

From time to time, as the years passed, we would say
'spaghetti bolognese' to him, shyly at first and then, as time
went on, more boldly. We said that if he ever felt like making
spaghetti bolognese we were first in the queue. We would set a
date, we said, or he could – days, months, even years ahead.
He smiled in an indulgent, slightly sad way.

'Sure,' he said, 'one day. When I'm in the mood.'

While we were waiting for the spaghetti bolognese his wife would cook for us.[1] Soups, stews, casseroles, roast meats, chicken paprika, noodles, goulash, home-made sausages, potatoes, mashed, boiled, fried or roasted with garlic, and sometimes roast goose with red cabbage. All these and more came out of her tiny kitchen. But I think we all felt that, good as they were, they were only a prelude. Because, as a rule, after we had tucked into goulash or paprika or spiced veal or a whole pike with sorrel sauce garnished with grilled vegetables and home-made noodles, and we were sitting around the table over a cup of coffee, John would smile wearily, put his hands to his head and say, 'One day, *one* day I will make you spaghetti bolognese. My spaghetti bolognese.'

'It is,' his wife would say appreciatively, 'absolutely brilliant!'

We said that if he thought it might be helpful, we would be prepared to go to market for him. *Just make a list*, we said. If he needed special pans or spices or cleavers flown in from the continent, we would be only too happy to supply them.

Eventually we gave up.

It seemed as if we were never going to get his spaghetti bolognese. As far as we could tell, he made it for other, luckier people than us. Some people over from America were given his spaghetti bolognese and had to be dragged out of the house by Group 4 Security as it was almost impossible to

1  My brother's wife is a Hungarian from the former Yugoslavia and is an excellent cook. She was brought up in the countryside near the Hungarian border where their idea of a Christmas treat was to allow a child to hold the pig's tail while they slaughtered it (the pig, not the child). At least peasant culture understands the importance of food. When John was teaching at the University of Novi Sad, a place now presumably given over to Serbian re-education, he was asked by one of the locals what the English said before they were about to eat. He was about to say 'For what we are about to receive, may the Lord make us truly thankful. Amen', but decided that no one in the United Kingdom said grace any more. He ended up by telling the man, a large Serbian called Bratko, that the English equivalent of *bon appétit* was 'Dig in!' Bratko obliged everyone by yelling this before starting all subsequent meals taken with my brother's wife.

separate them from the dish. A cousin came from Australia and broke her teeth on the saucepan while trying to lick it clean.

Then, one day, when we were round at his flat at about four in the afternoon, he emerged from the kitchen wearing an apron and carrying a wooden spoon. He had a holy, dedicated expression on his face. He looked as if he were about to set out on a pilgrimage of some sort. His wife turned to us, and with the sort of whisper which parents use to their children while viewing French cathedrals said, 'He's going to make spaghetti bolognese.'

We were not ready. We had eaten a bare six hours ago. We had not thought about this event. It was, we said, too big for us to contemplate. Couldn't we have a couple of weeks to think about it? And, surely, he was not simply going to go into the kitchen and make spaghetti bolognese, *his* spaghetti bolognese, just like that?

'He's been up all night,' she said. 'The mood came on him.' He went back into the kitchen wearing that expression you only ever see on the faces of men who are wearing aprons in their wife's kitchen. For some reason, I couldn't say why, it always makes me think of the word nappies.

Quite a lot of noise came out of the kitchen as we sat in his front room and the day died outside his basement windows. There was banging. And a hissing sound. There was a shriek of steel against steel or the dull thud of blade cutting into wood. We wondered, aloud, what spices, what amazing complexity of flavours and textures were being put together out there, and we tried to let his wife know how humble and how honoured we felt to be actually *in the flat* while he was making spaghetti bolognese. From time to time he would come out of the kitchen and stand with the wooden spoon held out before him like a sentry's rifle. He reminded me at these moments of a royal physician emerging to give hourly details of Her Majesty the Queen's labour. He hardly ever spoke. We would ask him how it was going and he would smile, enigmatically, give a brief weary shrug and with the exquisite practicality common among great artists, say, 'Okay' or 'Not so bad.'

Sometimes he came out and we could tell things were not going too well back there. Some element in the amazingly complicated blending process he was engaged in had gone wrong. Something was too salty; a tomato had turned out to be not quite up to par. But, although there were definite crises in the four or five hours that it took him to bring his spaghetti bolognese before the public, he never let us know what they were. He suffered out there alone. Eventually his wife went in to the rescue. She would only, she said, be doing menial stuff.

'When he's cooking,' she said, 'I just obey orders.'

There was clearly some delicate nuance of the dish that needed attention. Perhaps, we whispered, as the darkness came in and the lights flickered on in the street above, the pasta dough had not proved? He was, almost certainly, we felt, making the pasta himself. In fact some of us suggested that he was probably laying the eggs, growing the tomatoes and killing the cattle out there, since we had now been sitting in his front room for about the length of a transatlantic flight.[2]

When the dish finally came to table it looked, superficially, like the spaghetti bolognese palmed off on the unsuspecting public in places such as Ravenna or Milan. There was a dish of spaghetti that looked a little like the sort you get out of packets. There was a dish of sauce that looked like the meat sauce you see in restaurants everywhere. In fact, to be perfectly honest, there were some of us who at first thought we had been waiting all this time for something that was, well, to use the words of one of us, 'bog standard spag. bol.' When it came to forking the stuff into our mouths, too, I have to confess that there was a moment when we all felt we were going to be disappointed. The pasta, at first, tasted like pasta and the meat sauce, in the early stages of mastication, seemed just a lot of old mince fried up with onions and tomatoes and a few other bits of vegetable matter.

Gradually, though, as we swallowed more and more of it,

2   My wife records that, in the early 1980s, during the time it took me to chop one onion, she made a quiche lorraine, a mixed salad and cleaned and boiled three quarters of a pound of new potatoes.

we began to see the strengths and complexity of the flavours. Bit by bit as we chewed our way through yard after yard of spaghetti, we began to appreciate that what we were eating went far beyond food.

John was a great help here. I don't think any of us would have seen quite how superior his sauce and spaghetti were compared to the best that the world's chefs could do if he had not talked us through each mouthful so carefully.

'You see the delicate way it's herbed,' he'd say, while his wife shovelled the stuff into her mouth as if her life depended upon it. 'Notice the way the sauce sort of *gets into the meat*.' We said we had. The keener of us begged him to let us know how he did it. He smiled evasively. It wasn't a thing you talked about, even to close friends and family. One day, when he was old and tired, perhaps even close to death, he might pass on the recipe. But, for the moment, his lips were sealed.

I don't think I have ever felt obliged to eat as much spaghetti as I did that night. We licked our plates. We slurped the sauce out of the dish. We practically put it on to our hair and rubbed it into our scalps. And, when we staggered out at about two in the morning, stomachs distended, eyes glazed, brains incapable of coherent thought, he saw us off at the door with that same weary enigmatic expression.

'Now,' he said to us, 'you can say you really *have* had spaghetti bolognese.'

JP was not this kind of cook. By the time the lock-keeper had returned from taking his son to school and the first few cars had passed on the road on the other bank, he had managed to make and serve breakfast. The coffee was good. I savoured its sharpness as the noises of the morning grew louder. I said I would wash up. While JP rolled the awning up away from the metal hoops I packed away the rubbish from both meals, and by eight we were pulling the skiff into the lock.

From Chertsey, where the river flows under the M3 motorway, up past Laleham and Staines, the Thames runs among flat meadows. There are bungalows, then long stretches of fields in which cows are arranged, unromantically, against a background of distant roads. Here and there far away, factories shimmered in the summer haze. Beyond Laleham, on the west bank, is one of the marinas that have, since Jerome's day, more or less displaced the old boat houses.

As we rowed upstream (we had agreed to do half-an-hour shifts each) we agreed that there was something obscene about these places.

'Gin palaces,' said JP sternly, as we passed thirty or forty white-hulled launches. 'What *i*s the point of them?'

A gigantic cruiser the size of a small minesweeper pulled up behind us on the port side and a rush of water slapped against the side of the skiff. Sprawled out in the July sun on the aft deck was a girl in a bikini. At the helm was a man of about fifty, pot-bellied in large blue shorts, looking rather like Captain Bird's Eye in the fish fingers advert. His craft seemed equipped with almost every conceivable aid to communication.

'It's got radar!' said JP. 'Presumably for spotting skiffs in the fog.'

I told JP that Matthew Arnold was buried at Laleham. He did not seem interested in this. Once started on the subject of gin palaces he would not be shifted. It was a phrase, he said, that his father particularly used. I think, I told him, it was a word my father would have used as well. As we pulled up towards Runnymede we talked about our families.

JP's father sounded very like mine, although he was from Northern Ireland and mine was of Welsh parents, though born in the Midlands.[3] They were both great respecters of rules. Men who, like Jerome, George and Harris, wanted to live quiet decent lives and were both, in their different ways,

3   David ffrancon Williams was a modern languages master at Manchester Grammar School, and from the late 1940s until the 1960s the headmaster of Kilburn Grammar school, a school that produced quite a number of eminent pupils. Brent Council Education Department rewarded him for this service by turning it into a comprehensive. This, as far as I could see, consisted of placing a large notice board outside the school saying COMPREHENSIVE – after which all the teachers left. When, in the 1980s, I visited it with David Robbins, an ex-pupil, the only sign of culture in the place was a tattered notice on a board urging pupils to attend a rally about Namibia. It is now the Ismaelia Muslim Primary School in the care of Yousef Islam, or Cat Stevens as I still insist on calling him.

ground down by the institutions they served. They were both teachers, and both came from a climate in which pleasure was dangerously close to luxury and luxury dangerously close to sin. I recall the day I used the word 'bird' about a woman. My father, showing a concern for correct language that both patriarchs and feminists share said, 'That's not a word ever to use in front of your mother.'

Perhaps it is the puritanism of the late nineteenth century that makes Jerome's humour such a liberating force. When Jerome, Wingrave and Hentschel started to row on the river in the 1880s dressed in blazers on a Sunday, they were hissed at by the religious element.

Guilt of the religious kind seems to have blighted the lives of both our fathers and our grandfathers, I said to JP. Perhaps we shouldn't use phrases like 'gin palaces' any more. Perhaps, as Larkin said, we should all go down the long slide, free as bloody birds.

JP spoke too about his mother, the daughter of one of Germany's most eminent physicists, a friend of Hans Bethe and Einstein, whose work on the physics of the sun would have won him a Nobel prize had anyone at the time realised quite how important it was. JP's grandfather had managed to get all his family out of Nazi Germany. Once they were in England, one son had left for Australia to fight the Germans from there, while another had been interned by the British Government as a suspected enemy agent. JP looked across at the peaceful Thames, slapping at the green banks, and towards Runnymede where King John was supposed to have founded the Charter of English liberty.

'The truth is, Nige, he said, 'don't be fooled by rules. Our fathers were limited by rules. You're taken in by rules. My family only survived because they broke them. Rules are for idiots.'

This struck me with the sharpness associated with discovering home truths in middle age. It was too late, I realised, for me to understand it.

'Last night', he said, 'I could see you were worrying about mooring in the wrong place. You shouldn't worry about things like that. Only do things correctly if *you* think they're correct.'

I said I would try not to worry about rules. The first rule I was going to break, I said, was the rule that we each rowed for half an hour. I had been rowing for only twenty minutes, I said, and my hands were developing blisters. My neck felt as if someone had just injected it with concrete. JP said there was no fixed rule about how long we each rowed for. If I wished to, he said, smiling, I might row on for hours. There was no need to stop rowing just because I felt like it.

On the port bow another launch came up level with us. We were both agreeing that this was a particularly stupid way of seeing the river when the young man in charge of it leaned out and called over to us.

'That looks like hard work. D'you fancy a tow?'

# Nine

The ethics of rowing are curious. Jerome acknowledges at least two occasions when he, George and Harris were towed, but people on the river are still distinctly cagey about it. It goes on. In some circles it is openly discussed. After a few drinks, rowing men will admit they, or at least acquaintances of theirs, have been towed; but they are guarded on the subject. Exactly how *far* you have been towed (assuming you admit to having been towed in the first place) is a tricky business. It is obviously something that, in the wrong hands, could wreck the whole spirit of the river. If one didn't keep a careful watch on it every skiff, single and double, even *canoes*, would be pimping along Nickcroft Ait, waving tow-lines and leering invitingly at passing cabin cruisers. Sculls would become irrelevant.

The fact of the matter is this. Sometimes, if you have been rowing for three or four hours, upstream, in the blazing heat of a July morning, an offer of mechanical assistance can seem very welcome. But you must never, when approached by a gin palace, launch, barge or cruiser, break down and cry with relief in front of them. You must never ask how far they are going or babble things along the lines of how kind they are or how no one else on the river understands the agony that you are going through. Never say things like, 'Christ, yes, thanks, I'm knackered. It's so kind of you, I'm dead, I'm absolutely beat!'

You should let them know, by the way you carry yourself, that, although it might seem as if they are doing you a favour, it is, in fact, the other way round. They are dull little people, plodding up from Marlow to Oxford, with nothing but the steering to worry about. For them the river is no more than a means to an end. By allowing them to hitch their miserable rope to your boat you are letting them in on some ancient ritual. They have become part of the ceremony, whose origins lie way back beyond Jerome's day, whose history begins in the time when there was only good, honest English oak in the hands of good, honest English seafaring men.

I confess that I found it difficult to stifle my sobs of gratitude when this particular pleasure craft made us its offer. But JP, who was steering, saw the thing in the right perspective. 'What do you think?' he said. 'Is it ethical?'

I let the sweat trickle down on to my chest. Then I said I thought it probably was. The launch came across our prow and idled about us up river. Now I was closer to it I could see that the man in charge of it was not your usual pot-bellied gin-swilling oaf, got up in some ghastly parody of a royal naval official uniform. He was a bright, attractive young man who, if the cards of life had been dealt differently, would have been hard at the sculls, as we were. There was something, I decided, almost saintly about him. He had a rugged, open, honest look about him.

'How far are you going?' he asked.

'Oxford,' I said, before JP could reply.

I felt keen to spend more than just an hour or so in this young man's company. I wanted to get to know him better, to understand how he came to be here, looking across the lawn of Runnymede with Coopers Hill luminous in the July heat behind, in what looked like quite a useful little motor boat.

He said he and his two friends had hired the boat for the day. This struck me as a decent, sensible sort of thing to have done.

'We could take you as far as Windsor.'

JP got out the Nicholson's Guide. While he was wondering, out loud, about the whole business of towing and airing some of the important issues discussed above, I crawled to the prow of the boat and, simpering at the man's two companions,[1] flung out our tow-line.

'Nice day,' said the young man.

I thought this a brilliant, concise and potentially profound remark.

The young man tied us up, smiling slightly in a way that inspired total confidence. He was a muscular lad of about 25, stripped to the waist, suggesting that he might be somebody who worked in the open air. But an artist of some kind too. Possibly, I thought, a landscape gardener or a manual labourer who wrote poetry. He seemed to combine physical and mental grace in a way that I could not remember having seen before.

My feelings for him were intensified when the tow-line snapped taut and we started to glide through the water. He had, I thought, a sort of heroic quality as he stood at the wheel scanning the river ahead, and Runnymede slid away behind our port bow. I waved brightly at him. Our prow bounced against the wash from his boat. Then there was the beginnings of Old Windsor on our port side as we swept up through the Ait that runs past Old Windsor Weir and on to the edge of Windsor Home Park.

'You all right?' said JP, as we tied up at Old Windsor Lock, tidily floating in behind the launch with the ease of a swan in motion.

'Fine!' I said. 'Fine!'

The young man turned out to be an estate agent.

I must confess that, previously, I have not had a high opinion of estate agents; but he was an exception to the rule. Property

1   I think, although I am not entirely sure, that they were both Swedish. But, in fact, only one of them may have been Swedish. Although three of my plays have been translated into Swedish, and I have had several cordial relations with Swedish writers and translators, even when talking to them I cannot rid myself of the feeling that I am talking to a distant, rather strict relative.

values are not always an interesting topic for discussion, but in his hands they became something exciting – not new territory, admittedly, but always interesting.

'A two-bedroom house in Staines,' he said, as I watched our two boats rise up the lock, 'is beyond belief. Prices are ridiculous.'

I looked lovingly at the rope that tied our two craft together – a symbol (I thought) of co-operation between different forces on the river, and tried to take in the depth and complexity of what he had just said. When the lock gates opened and we jerked to life behind the launch and started to slide up towards Datchet, JP said to me, 'Are you frightened he will cast us adrift or something?'

I thought it rather low of him to have spotted this.

My attempts to charm people are based on the fact that I think they may turn nasty at any moment. If JP maintained this high-level analysis of my behaviour, I decided, I might let him write the book. We try to take care not to let other people see revealing or shameful things about us but, in spite of ourselves, we wear them on our faces every day. No one finds you out as quickly as a travelling companion, not even a wife or brother.

On the port side, a huge barrier had been put up on the bank. It said NO MOORING. Windsor Castle's phoney turrets, the stone the grey of a posh private school uniform, rose above the trees about a mile or so away. Perhaps the royals were frightened that armies of paparazzi might moor secretly and swarm up on to the bank like weasels, scurrying across the fields towards Prince Andrew and his pals.[2]

2   Windsor is, indeed, a sinister place. While we were on the river, a woman on a pleasure barge told me that her vessel had been set adrift while she and her husband were asleep just above Windsor Lock. 'Who knows what might have happened if we hadn't woken up in time?' the woman told me. 'We might well have drifted towards the weir.' The fact that weirs are almost all protected by large wooden piles, that her boat was around thirty feet in length and would under no circumstances have slipped through the barrier, is irrelevant. Clearly the fear of the stern of one's vessel upending is an ancestral one and not based on reason. Interestingly enough, one of the few recorded personal anecdotes about

There is something insolent about the way private property meets the world we all have to share. Whenever I see the sign ANY BICYCLES ATTACHED TO THESE RAILINGS WILL BE REMOVED outside some property in London I want to rush into the nearest cycle shop, buy triple strength high tension locks and chain my bike to the steel fence so hard it will take the swine five hours with the local fire brigade before they can unglue so much as one wheel off their stupid bloody railings.

On the river, a collision of the private and the public is so shocking that it needs even more careful staging. Those who travel by water look in on the private lives of those rich and poor – their lives are briefly on display for you with all the touching incompleteness of a domestic scene observed from a moving train. The people who feel they need the reassurance of barbed wire or menacing signs warning you off their property arouse the Viking in all but the most timid of the crew of passing boats.

I was muttering something about Fergie as the launch ahead of us slowed. On the starboard bank was Eton College. We were at Romney Lock. The launch went into neutral and one of the young man's companions, a girl of about sixteen, leaned over the stern ready to untie our tow-line. Our skiff, still under way, ran for their stern. With the oars shipped, there was very little we could do to stop her. The girl bent over the stern of their boat, and before JP or I could warn her that the whole skiff, with us and all our gear aboard, was too heavy for anyone to check, she had reached desperately for our tow-line. The prow drove her hand into the stern of their launch. She screamed and both her companions bent over her.

I still don't know how badly she was hurt. While we shouted our sympathy they put the boat round and headed back for Windsor as fast as they could. As they passed us the young

Jerome on the river tells of George sculling towards a weir. On seeing a sign which said DANGER: WEIR AHEAD, Jerome remarked to George, 'Scull on. Such signs are only put up to frighten children and old women.'

man in charge of the boat told us not to worry. But he looked worried.

JP and I pulled in below the lock and reflected upon the unfairness of life. How often is kindness rewarded in just this way?[3] When the good Samaritan got to the next town he was probably beaten up as a troublemaker. Contact with people, even when you are doing them a favour, can open you up to danger.

We both got quite heated about this as we took the skiff through the lock. 'Anyway,' said JP, 'you've saved yourself half an hour's rowing.'

Our shift system had collapsed. Or, rather, I suspect that both of us were engaged in the game of polite man's bluff, often played by Englishmen who want, in the nicest possible way, to lumber each other.

'I don't know . . .' I said, as the skiff bobbed up in the surging water, JP holding on to the chain. 'How long did I do . . . ?'

'I'm not *sure* . . .'

There was a brief pause. Then JP added in a 'hell, I know this isn't the truth but you are obviously desperate and may have to head for the intensive care unit of the local hospital if you go on for any longer' sort of way, 'Probably, er . . . I don't know . . . er . . . nearly half an hour, I'm sure.'

'I'm just not sure,' was my response.

'No,' said JP.

As the lock gates opened, and the boat ahead of us went out towards the green levels of Windsor racecourse, we idled a little in the now calm water of the lock. The sun felt hot on my neck.

'I'll carry on as long as necessary, really!' I sounded cheerful

---

3  The most grievous example of this I can recall took place when a John Lewis delivery man attempted to release my Citroën GSA Estate from the bumper of the car parked behind it, where it had been trapped by the Citroën's suspension. During the course of the operation his forefinger became trapped between the bumpers of the two cars and he had to be taken to a local hospital for emergency surgery. All acts of charity can endanger both giver and recipient: as in the case of the late Robert Maxwell and the National Westminster Bank.

about this, but my expression was intended to leave JP in no doubt as to who would be directly responsible should the crash unit not get to my cardiac arrest in time.

'No, no, no, no, no,' he said, 'I think you *did* do half an hour.' He settled to the sculls. 'Anyway,' he went on, 'I think we should both do just about as long as we feel we can.'

'Absolutely.'

'I'm going to do fifteen minutes,' he said.

We both laughed then and with a large cigar clamped between his teeth JP pulled us up towards Boveney Lock. I pointed out that on the bank on the starboard bow we might well be able to find *trifolium fragiferum*, or strawberry clover, the fruiting heads of which resemble strawberries in shape and colour. This didn't seem to strike a chord with him.

I went on to tell him that one or two of our largest native grasses were to be found in this part of the river, or at least they were at the time when the Nicholson's Guide from which I was reading was published, that is after the end of decimalisation and towards the beginning of the all-number telephone system. He grunted at this. I took this as encouragement and reminded him that *glyceria maxima* (great reed grass) can stand up to eight feet in height, while *phragmites* (reed), which can be even taller, has shaggy, silky flower tassels and a softer purple colour. He grunted again as he clicked the sculls through the rowlocks and, watching his stroke carefully, engaged each blade in the current. When each stroke was finished, he ran the sculls back close to the water – now brown, now green, now dark steely blue – and eased them back into the stream.

'Look!' I said, pointing to a line of grasses by a mess of small bushes against which the river slopped like beer in an overfilled glass. 'Look there! *Carex ripara* or great pond sedge! Three feet high and flowers in early spring!'

JP said it wasn't early spring. It is very difficult to interest a man actually engaged in the practice of rowing, in the beauties of nature that are all around him. As we covered the two miles from Boveney to Bray he only really became animated when telling me about a large blister that was developing on his bum.

I tried to look concerned about this. 'Whereabouts is it?' I said, sympathetically. 'Left or right buttock?' He did not seem to be very precise about this. I studied him carefully and gained the impression that he was definitely coming down less heavily on the starboard side of his rear end.

'It's on the right, isn't it?' I said. 'Or rather on *your* left. Your port buttock will be perceived by me as my starboard buttock.'

He said, rather irritably, that without getting out a mirror and mooning at the fishermen seated on both banks either side of us he could not be sure. We paused in mid-stream just below Bray. In the aft locker I found something a little like a whoopee cushion which was, apparently, designed for just this purpose. He went back to it manfully, but after a while the sight of a man hopping from one cheek to another muttering and cursing to himself was too much for me. I took the sculls from him. As I wrapped my hands around them I noticed that I too had blisters. Mine were on the palms of both hands.

Suppose we didn't get through to Alan that night? Suppose he didn't get the message I had left from Shepperton? Suppose he was headed, inexorably, for Marlow? How were we going to stop him?

It was about four or five in the afternoon. We were seven miles below Marlow with only one pair of workable buttocks between us. This was a crisis, in my view, comparable with the loss of all pitons a thousand feet up some over-subscribed Himalayan peak. With a conviction that things depended on me, I dug the sculls into the river, and pulled hard.

# Ten

*Truth telling and the art of writing – More thoughts on propulsion of river-going craft – Difficulties facing modern man – A grandmother's stern convictions – Thoughts on happiness and its implementation.*

Honesty, some would say, is inimical to good writing.

In spite of Jerome's bold declaration, in his foreword to the 1889 edition of *Three Men in a Boat*, that he had simply set down the events of his epic trip as they happened, we have hard evidence that in certain cases Jerome was economical with the truth.[1] Most lovers of the book will recall the passage

---

1   The question of the accuracy of Jerome's account of his holiday would obviously be crucial to any serious scholarly study of his work. We know, from his autobiography and from the posthumous biography, that *Three Men in a Boat* is a record not of one trip but a collation of memories of several such expeditions. But the assumption taken by Jerome's 1981 biographer Connolly that Jerome actually went on the journey he described cannot be substantiated. This line of enquiry leads us to a question as important as 'Was D H Lawrence a woman?' or 'Who really wrote the Essays of Virginia Woolf?'

    In an attempt to try and substantiate the reality of 'Hentschel' and 'Wingrave' the author contacted all Hentschels and Wingraves listed in the London telephone directory. There are five Wingraves and two Hentschels. Nearly all the Wingraves were out apart from a lady who told me her grandfather had worked on the Canadian Pacific railway, and asked if this was of interest for my book. One of the Hentschels told me that Carl Hentschel, the Harris of the book, had two children, one of whom was the first principal of Surrey University. The other was Irene Hentschel, a theatrical producer who married the author, Ivor Brown.

where the author describes Harris being chucked out from almost every pub in South London. The joke about Harris's drinking was, it transpires, a joke at the expense of the reader. For Hentschel was, as all of Jerome's associates knew, the only teetotaller of the party. Jerome, as we have seen, lied through his teeth about the dog. It is possible that he was lying about far more than that.

It is possible that George Wingrave never turned up at all, or, if he did turn up, that he did not bring a banjo. It is entirely probable that they remembered the tin-opener. It is possible that the whole tin-opener business is an elaborate joke at the reader's expense, as Jerome was known among his friends as a stickler for precision, and that late one night in their club Hentschel or Wingrave said, 'Wouldn't it be frightfully funny if J and the rest of us forgot the tin-opener?'

It may well be this fact that gives the business of forgetting the tin-opener its distinctive authenticity. There is nothing so uninspiring as the truth, nothing so dull as accurately reported fact.

It is just conceivable that Jerome never went on the river at all. That the whole business of 'going on the river' was something he heard about in some pub, and that 'Wingrave' and 'Hentschel' were fragments of the man's busy imagination.

The fact of the matter is, I suppose, the more closely you try to examine Jerome the more elusive he becomes. In spite of the boasting about his famous acquaintances in his autobiography, it seems no one really thought Jerome was worth discussing. His natural daughter, who died childless, is as much a mystery as was his wife. There are no intimate letters, no press scandals (apart from a libel case which cost Jerome thousands of pounds and took him years to repay[2]), and no mystery. His autobiography exposes the small tragedy

Both marriages were, childless.

2   The libel case was caused by an article in *Today* on which Jerome was an editor. Although the parties settled, Jerome's costs were £11,000 – a staggering sum by the standards of the day. He and the plaintiff agreed that the best thing they could do for each other was to strangle the other one's lawyer.

of his life then lets it fall, unconsidered. He is a face in the crowd, a young, anonymous man of the Edwardian era, who led a decent unadventurous life and survived perhaps only because he immortalised ordinariness.

*And in order to do so he had to take liberties with the truth.*

I make these remarks in a spirit intended to mark a new openness between myself and the reader because, sooner or later, although I have been avoiding it, using philosophy, anecdotes and all the apparatus of *belles lettres*, I am going to have to tell you how JP and I managed to get from Shepperton to Cookham in just one day.

It is a secret that neither of us has until now shared with even those closest to us. It is something that I do not like to entrust even now to the page in front of me. JP telephoned me some twenty minutes or so ago, and I sensed a certain tension in his voice as he asked me, 'How is the book going?' Exactly how much of what was said between us in that intense few days as we rowed up from Hampton Wick was I going to reveal?

Well – and only now as I write this am I discovering the fact – there are certain things I cannot lie about. There really is such a person as John Paul Davidson. He is 5 feet 10 inches, weighs 12 stone, is married and until dissuaded from so doing by his wife, was on the verge of calling his eldest son Finbar. He danced a traditional Javanese rain dance *in a kilt* at his wedding. I, too, am real. My full name is Henry Nigel Williams, and the photo on the jacket of this book, while flattering to a certain degree, is a rough approximation of how I actually look. I was born in 1948. I too weigh 12 stone, and my dog is a real dog.

Now the confession I have to make to you. John Paul Davidson and myself were *towed* from somewhere near Bray to Cookham. If you add our second tow to the first (from Laleham to Datchet) you will realise that we managed to get scorched buttocks, blistered hands and a double hernia apiece from the equivalent of rowing about three and a half miles. If you want the truth I must confess that the real title of this book should be *Being Towed up the River* or *Nancying about*

*behind Motorised Craft in the Thames Valley.* At some point in
our apology for a journey a group of young people came to
the edge of the bank and yelled at us, 'I could run faster than
that mate!'

At the time both of us got irritated about this remark. We
speculated about the broken homes from which these youths
obviously came. We were even hardhearted about their obvious deprivation. They didn't deserve any of the help offered
by a modern state, we muttered, if all they could think to do
with their leisure time was to come down to the water's edge
and hurl abuse at two young men for not rowing fast enough.

But we were not young men. The combined age of the
boat at this stage (if you include Badger) was 87 years old.
We were pathetic specimens, not worthy of calling ourselves
rowing men. Gone are the days when men would push their
boats on *rollers* up past the weir, or when Jerome, George
and Harris would row their craft for miles at a time. The
Thames Jerome wrote about is dead. The boat houses are
gone – as surely as are the years that separate us from
Jerome, George and Harris. No one wears blazers to go
boating. Women don't fuss as they did in Jerome's day over
the state of their long muslin dresses. No one *really* talks about
'rowing men'. All the games we play these days are imitation
games.

You may think I am making too much of being towed but,
being towed can seem as fatal a sin as Adam's nibbling an apple.[3] Our second tow happened in this manner. JP was rowing

3   JP himself is still a little cagey about the fact that we were towed. He is,
    like the author Redmond O'Hanlon, a born traveller. Sometimes when
    talking to both him and O'Hanlon, I wonder whether either of them
    have ever been further than Didcot. I can only suggest to both of them
    that each lodges his air tickets in a Swiss bank against the day when a
    biography comes to be written.
        Reality is not of primary concern in a literary text, of course, especial-
    ly when, as in travel literature, the genre's power depends almost totally
    on its pretensions to authenticity. The author William Boyd once told me
    that he was commissioned to write a travel book about driving across
    America. He cannot drive and his wife, throughout the trip, was at the
    wheel. This did not prevent the man Boyd, when at the typewriter, from

when what looked like a Henley launch sneaked up behind us. Now I think about it, the man driving had a Mephisthophelean appearance: a big, handsome face, large nose, expressive eyes and the ways of a man of the world. Perhaps rowers who have fallen give off a tell-tale scent. The stranger came astern of us and smiled across at JP.

'Warm work!' he said.

'It is!' said JP, giving a brave little smile. Then he plied the sculls. As he pulled them back through the water, he gave a little cry of distress.

'Are you okay?' said the stranger.

'He's fine,' I said. 'I'll give him a dry biscuit if he gets us to Marlow by lunchtime.'

JP sculled again. This time he groaned quite shamelessly.

'I think I'll be okay . . .' he said, sounding like a man who has just had his appendix out, 'although . . .' He let this sentence hang in the air. Before he could start publicly describing the condition of his buttock, I said, 'He's pretty fit. He's been up Everest.'

They seemed impressed by this; but JP let out a cry that made it clear that what he was suffering now was far worse than anything that had been dished out by the upper slopes of the Himalayas.

The man in the launch and his friend were now looking

using phrases like 'I gunned the big engine as I turned to Highway 66' and 'I felt the wheel respond as I took the huge Packard into the fast lane' etc. The best travel writers are, surely, those who re-invent places they have visited to suit their own imaginations. One author I know divides travel books into two kinds – those that make you wish you had been on the trip and those that make you glad you stayed at home. I would argue that the journey is of less importance than the person undergoing it. We read Lawrence on New Mexico, not because we want to find out what the scenery is like, but because, whether he is writing about pornography, the novels of Thomas Hardy or peasants on the other side of the world, he is a vivid writer. The most telling illustration of the act that it is not necessary to go anywhere to write a travel book was given to me by a Scottish writer who has recently completed a book about Peru. 'My most important source', he told me, 'was not my experience of the place but The Ladybird *Book of Peru*.'

really worried. Before JP had a chance to tell him his left leg was a recent acquisition from the Roehampton artificial limb centre or that rowing up the Thames was his way of getting over by-pass heart surgery, I said to the couple, 'He's all muscle, he can go for hours. And it's only the start of his shift.'

But by now the man was waving the line. JP scurried forward with the speed and grace of a gazelle. He threw the man in the launch our tow-line and began a conversation. The man and his wife, it appeared, were going to Henley for the regatta. JP sounded keenly interested by this. The boat wasn't a *real* Henley launch but a fibre glass replica of one. As the man tied our tow-line to his stern JP commented on the quietness of the engine, the beauty of the vessel's line and the way in which this particular small craft was, unlike your average gin palace, in *harmony* with the river.

I found all this rather disgusting. The man was giving us a tow. There was no need to go on all fours to him. I sat back in the steering seat and busied myself with Nicholson's Guide.

'This,' said JP as our prow bounced through the water at the end of a quivering rope, 'is the life.'

'It's the shame I can't stand,' I said as the sun glistened on the steel-blue water, lined with birch, oak and poplar. Over to our right a group of ducks sat, proprietorially, on somebody's lawn. Over to our left a swan, one of the creatures of the animal kingdom best qualified to convey disdain, cruised the shoreline. Up in the sky three-decker clouds, built out of bruised blue and cotton wool white, drifted over the home counties.

'It's the guilt.'

JP said I should stop feeling guilty.

As our skiff glided, illicitly, up towards Boulter's Lock, I said, 'It's the lazy man's way.'

That was a phrase of my grandmother's. My grandparents do not include anyone as interesting as JP's, although my mother's father, who was Chief Education Officer for Salford, acquired, in his daughter's eyes at any rate, a certain glamour. My maternal grandmother was born a farmer's daughter in the Lake District. I recall being shown a Diorama in some exhibition at a museum. It contained dummies in linens and calico stooped over wooden workbenches and spinning-wheels. There were antique tools and porcelain of the kind not easily available in the 1950s. It seemed to me to belong to another century altogether. My mother told me it was a model of a wheelwright's shop, and that my grandmother had owned just such a shop.

Jenny Hartley, as she was called, ended her days in the front room of our house in Mill Hill in North London, being persecuted by her grandchildren. She was as much part of Jerome's world as non-conformist morality or pretty dresses in an open boat. One of her favourite phrases was 'It's the lazy man's way.'[4]

*The lazy man's way*. I think she probably regarded tin-openers as a cop-out. She would rather have had us gnawing our way through the metal. Her particular scorn was reserved for firelighters. Firelighters were, she felt, somehow effeminate. The idea that you could just sling a few strips of treated cotton wool on to a pile of coal, flick on a match and let it suddenly catch light, was somehow repulsive. A fire was started by rolling endless newspapers into spills, adding about a kilo of brushwood then balancing small coal carefully around the grate. It was supposed to take three hours. A firelighter helping you

---

4   Towards the end of her life my grandmother would often head out for a meeting with her cousin Hannah, who had been dead for nearly thirty-five years. I can still remember her putting on her hat and coat and walking out of the door with her stick to see this deceased relative. Indeed, Hannah is as real to me if not more so, than many other of my relatives. My grandmother's favourite habit in her nineties was to sit on the sofa with a copy of *The Times* looking away from it at regular intervals to say, 'Nothing but wars and rumours of wars.' Almost the only other thing she said during this period was, 'Weary I am and laden with my sin, I look to heaven and long to enter in.' When she moved from her sitting room to the kitchen, a distance of some ten or fifteen yards, she farted, sometimes for periods as long as one minute and forty seconds. I was surprised, when shown pictures of her as a young girl, that she was particularly beautiful.

    My paternal grandmother was Welsh.

on your way was an impostor. Human guilt has not changed since John Bunyan's day.

'Less is more,' said JP as he lit another cigar, adding, 'relax!'

I did relax in the end. I lay back in the steering seat, took a glass of red wine from JP and, trailing my hand in the water, gave myself up to the sun. To happiness. We have been made to feel guilty about happiness for too long. Happiness, someone is always trying to suggest, is at someone else's expense. It is as if we have been taught to think that there is a finite amount of happiness in the world. As if happiness were like lead or copper or iron or some other non-renewable mineral resource we should be depressed about having so little of.

For years I went around pretending I wasn't happy. It seemed, somehow, the right thing to do. Happiness seemed so dull somehow. 'How are things?' people would say. 'Oh,' I would reply, 'all right. You know. . . .' To confess you were actually happy was to call down the wrath of the gods. To imply that you got out of bed in the morning and thought, 'Great! Another day!' was to own up to being an unfeeling swine untouched by the misery of the world.

But if someone can't be happy, what is there left for the lonely, the sick, the afraid or even the merely neurotic? Happy people should be like a distant light for such poor spirits, a voice from far away that seems to say, 'It can get better. It is getting better. It will get better.'

My youngest son is happy. He is, people say, like me, and he is happy in the way I was happy as a child; his brothers have spotted this in him and they don't approve of it. Because, of course, happiness is in part a matter of being absolutely clueless. I remember feeling happy as a child about the fact that I was 'rather good' at cricket. It wasn't until I actually got out on to the pitch standing there in my pads and with my bat at the ready and was clean bowled by the first ball, that I realised that my 'rather good' was a wish rather than a fact. But happy people deal in wishes rather than facts. And the truly happy person is so stupid that once he has realised that wishes don't come true he sets about accommodating himself to precisely that fact. Happiness is not anything like triumph or ecstasy

or satisfaction, or any of the traditional qualities with which it
has been confused. Happiness in the end is about accepting
your limitations. About having the grace and good sense to
recognise that there are some things that you will never do
and some things that you will never enjoy, but that while you
are accepting your limitations there will always be that tree
to look at, that cloudscape to study, that glass of wine to roll
around your tongue.

The happiest person I ever met was a taxi driver in West
London. 'Every day,' he said to me, 'I get up and take the cab
out. I drive around and pick up fares till about eleven. Then
I have a sandwich. Then I drive and take people around until
about two.' I assumed he was going to go on to tell me how
he really wanted to be a conductor of the London Symphony
Orchestra or how his wife had left him for the man next door,
but he did not. 'At about two,' he went on, 'I have my lunch,
which is usually a sandwich. And I have it . . . in the cab!' He
seemed particularly pleased about this.

'Then,' he went on, 'I go back to driving. I drive around and
pick up fares and carry on with that until about six or seven in
the evening when I stop again for a break. Usually in the form
of a sandwich.' I was beginning to feel devastated by the waste
of a human life that was being laid out before me. It seemed,
somehow, so bleak. So desolate. Just drive, drive, drive and
every few hours a sandwich. What was the point of it all?

'At about eight or nine,' he went on, 'I go back to the wife
and we have our evening meal.'

*Don't tell me – it's a giant sandwich.*

'Usually,' he continued, 'a cooked meal of some description.
Then we watch television. Which I find very interesting. Then
we go to bed.'

Yes? With your next door neighbour, *I hope*! I was leaning
forward out of my seat waiting for the punch line. I was waiting
for him to start telling me about the futility of it all, the loneliness, the pointless driving from one place to another, the hard
faces of the people, the lack of real human sympathy or trust.

'Then', he said, 'next day it all starts all over again.' He
paused. Now, I thought, we are going to get it.

'It's a good life,' he said finally. 'I think of myself as a completely happy man.'

What a moron! He drives a taxi all day, eats a few sandwiches and he's happy! What an idiot! Isn't there anything else in life?

But you can't stop happy people. A hundred years after the publication of *Three Men in a Boat* people have forgotten Jerome. They have forgotten the fact that his mother and father were desperately in love with each other, or that his mother prayed every night that her hopeless husband could have some success in business. They have forgotten that Jerome enlisted as an ambulance driver in the First World War at the age of fifty and more, and that the experience killed him. They have forgotten that he wrote an autobiographical novel called *Paul Kelver*, which he thought of as his masterpiece, but which no one nowadays can read. All they remember is that a hundred years or so ago three young men went out on a river and forgot a tin-opener. And people still do go on the river in spite of the war that damaged Jerome and killed thousands of the young men his daughter might have married. People still go down to the river, row up through Shepperton and Chertsey, Pangbourne and Goring to Oxford, and find, in spite of everything, that they can be happy. Perhaps it is because of that that people remember Jerome and his one great book.

'This', said JP, as he lit another cigar, 'is complete and utter bliss!'

He blew out a cloud of smoke on the water and as dusk fell we cruised up through Cliveden Woods[5] where huge beech

5 Cliveden Wood is perhaps the first truly 'rural' stretch of the river Thames, perhaps because it is owned by the National Trust. The river bank on the Cliveden House side is marked by phoney Tudor cottages and large National Trust signs warning the punter that mooring is not free. This is not the place to rehearse the well-known story of the Profumo affair or of the luck of the Astor family, but perhaps it might be interesting to recall that David Astor once told a friend of a friend of the author's that he was 'astounded' to learn that several of his employees did not actually own their own houses. We are closer to the nineteenth century than we imagine.

and chestnut trees rise steeply up to the house that was once the home of the Astors. Clouds of midges fought with each other under the darkening trees that leaned down in the evening and the water lay, calmly, all about us.

'And every second that passes', JP went on, 'is bringing us closer and closer to Alan.'

# Eleven

*We become wild men – Our diet and appearance – We moor near Cookham – How Stanley Spencer's village has changed – Thoughts on catering – We make contact with the third man – Au pairs and their habits.*

On the other side of Cliveden Reach shame overtook us. We said good-bye to the Henley launch. As we did so, the driver's companion, in reaching out for our tow-line, was stung by a wasp. 'We're cursed,' said JP. 'We are the bringers of Death!'

Slowly and thoughtfully we rowed through the lock, along the cut that leads to Cookham weir. The darkness had come down on the river and as we rowed past the Ferry Inn, we lowered our voices as if out of respect for the silence in the fields beyond the village.

We discussed Alan's arrival or, at least, getting nearer to a telephone that would connect us to Alan's answering machine. We moored just above Cookham. It was dark by the time the boat was secure and the two of us walked back into the village. There were boats moored every few yards. In one cabin cruiser, an entire family were grouped around the television. In another, a sedate-looking young couple washed dishes. The names of the boats – *Fair Minstrel, Watership Down, Maid of the Isles*, or even the wilder efforts *Yohar, Just Groovin* – could not conceal their drab domesticity.

'I'm a water gypsy!' we could hear their owners say as they parked neatly and tidily, hung up their washing and turned their eyes away from the lights above the weir or the dark water by the bridge.[1]

We were not one of them. We ate Marks & Spencer coronation chicken straight out of the packet, standing up, in rough fields in the darkness. Compared to them we were Vikings, animals, and as we came into Cookham JP said in a fairly authentic Norse voice, 'We find women now. Bring them back to the boat.'

There were quite a lot of women in Cookham; but none of them looked as if they might be keen on accompanying two middle-aged men back to their camping skiff. They were shrieking with laughter in the pub or slamming the doors of expensive cars as their boyfriends drove off into the dark lanes of the country.

Some of them were wearing uniforms designed by whoever is in charge of these things at Trust House Forte. The local pub was one of the Beefeater chain which is run by THF. There were neat skirts and blouses for the girls, cheeky waistcoats for the boys and, pinned on each blouse, a little badge telling you what the person in the clothes was called. Derek. Norman. Sheila. The whole idea was, presumably, to let you know that, behind the hand that carries your burger and chips across the floor to you, there was a *person*.[2]

One of these people was serving behind the bar developing a relationship with a thickset young man in his early twenties. Perhaps, suggested JP, there were Beefeater training schools where, along with uniform and the badge, you got a crash course in how to spend twenty minutes pulling a pint of lager.

1 The metal bridge at Cookham is comparatively recent (it post-dated our Nicholson's Guide), but, like a great many of the new bridges over the Thames, is architectually pleasing to the eye.

2 Cookham was, of course, the place where Stanley Spencer lived and worked, and the waterside pub referred to in this chapter appears in Spencer's picture *Christ at Cookham Regatta* which, although only half finished, still shows this unique artist's talent for reproving and endorsing his all-too-human subjects. It shows the landlord of the Ferry Inn (not at the time, needless to say, owned by Trust House Forte), watching the regatta with pleasure, while, in another part of the picture, Christ's figure redeems his Brueghel-like home counties peasants.

'That was lager, was it?' the barperson was saying.

'That's right,' said the thickset young man. 'A pint of lager.'

'A pint or a half?'

'A pint.'

'*Right!*' murmured the barperson and moved with some decisiveness towards the glasses on the shelf behind him. Then he stopped, trapped in that ghastly no-man's land between receiving an order and having to carry it out.

'Of . . . lager, you said?'

'That's right!' said the young man. 'A pint of lager.'

The customer seemed to be enjoying this. *I don't mind how long I wait,* his expression seemed to say, *just carry on talking to me, experiencing me as a person, and I'll be fine.* Perhaps this was a little ritual the two of them had – some fragment of the law of the old English local that had once stood on the site of this place. Perhaps he was less interested in the drink than in managing to exchange a few words with the barperson.

'And', went on the thickset youth, 'an orange juice and lemonade please.' This set the barperson thinking. He abandoned all attempts to get to grips with the pint of lager. This was clearly something that drink-supplier and customer were really going to have to chat over together before anyone got within ten yards of a beer pump.

'You mean,' said the barperson with sudden, fierce intelligence, 'orange juice and lemonade mixed *in the same glass?*'

'That's it!' said the thickset young man cheerfully.

I now decided that these two were obviously in some kind of conspiracy together. They had been at school together in Cookham. And this is something they dreamed up together in the playground.

'A St Clement's,' said the barperson.

'If you like . . .'

'Some people call it that,' said the barperson and went off to look for the necessary bottles.

The thickset young man let his friend get to the shelf before he said, 'And a rum and coke, please, with the lager.'

The barperson had forgotten all about the lager. There was a wail of panic from behind the bar.

'Oh my God!' They were both on familiar ground now.

'Was it a pint? Or a half?'

'Actually,' said the youth cheerfully, 'it *was* a pint but I think I'll make it a half.'

'I think,' said JP, 'this is a bring–your–sleeping bag sort of local.'

'It is,' said a man directly behind. 'It's the bloody first circle of hell, this is!'

The barperson was busy with the lager, giving it a lot of quality time. When it was finally set on the bar in front of the young man the crowd behind him all sighed with communal relief. But, if we thought that at last things were moving we were wrong. The thickset young man went on to order four more pints of lager. Each pint was asked for and served individually. He clearly liked each one to come as a surprise. Then he ordered four more halves of lager and two bitter shandies. He went on, apparently having forgotten about the rum and coke, to request a gin and tonic, a dry sherry, a medium sherry with ice and a glass of red wine. The barperson nodded during this recital and then, immediately, forgot it and got the young man to repeat each item of the order. Occasionally the thickset young man would throw in a new drink just to confuse things, and the whole business would start all over again. I looked round the pub but could see no group of people large enough to fit the young man's order. Perhaps, JP said, we were on *Beadle's About* and, at any moment, a television crew would spring through the doors and offer us all free drinks.

Somehow, in the middle of all this, some poor soul, crazed with thirst, stole up to the bar and made off with the original half of lager. It is possible that he didn't want to drink it; that, as the original building block of what must by now be the longest, slowest, most amazingly ill-administered drinks order in the history of catering, it was of antiquarian interest. Perhaps he was going to put it in some Beefeater museum, where they record their famous victories over the consumer.

## THE ORIGINAL 'HALF OF LAGER' IN THE HISTORIC 'COOKHAM WAIT'

would find pride of place next to

## UNDELIVERED SCAMPI, *c.* 1933. THOUGHT TO BE FROM THE FAMOUS 'EAST MIDLANDS' HOARD

'I think,' said the thickset young man, 'there's a half of lager missing . . .' There was obviously no question of just pulling another one. That had simplicity and directness about it that was not for him. Instead he instigated a large-scale search, enlisting the help of people on both sides of the bar.

'Has anyone,' he said, 'seen a half of lager?'

Quite a few locals wanted to join in on this one. Several people said they thought they had seen a half of lager. One man said he had seen it on a radiator in the far corner of the room. An old lady suggested it might be on one of the tables outside, overlooking the river. A middle-aged man swore blind there never had been a half of lager, that it was a phantom lager, while a woman of about his age immediately to my left insisted that it had always been a pint. I began to think that they might *be all in on it*.

Now that the pint/half issue had been opened up again, the barperson engaged with enthusiasm and asked the young man whether he really wanted a half or a pint. And, if he wanted a half, whether he would like the original half traced, or whether he would like a new half drawn. If, on the other hand, he wanted a pint, would he rather have it in a jug, a straight-sided glass or some other form of domestic utensil? Before the young man had the chance to request a plastic bucket or a chamber pot or a silver replica of the leaning tower of Pisa I heard myself screaming. I can't remember precisely what it was. Something about dying of thirst and loneliness, about a hot day rowing on the river, and the desperate need for a cool pint of English ale.

The bar went very quiet. Somewhere over to my left a small

fat man in traditional Beefeater costume said, 'Excuse me, Sir. Is that your dog?'

The mood of the locals was turning nasty. 'There we were,' their faces seemed to say, 'enjoying a quiet queue, and you have to come along and spoil it with your posh London ways. We like waiting for our drinks down here in Cookham. It's part of the traditional rhythm of village life.'

'It is,' I said.

'Would you please take it outside?' said the man sharply. 'It's a hygiene question.'[3]

I started to twitch. JP laid a soothing hand on my arm. 'Come on,' he said. 'We'll phone Alan, then we'll have a drink.' We went out to the telephone and called Alan. We didn't get his machine but his male au pair, although JP pointed out that we might have got more sense out of his machine.[4]

Nobody knows where Alan got his au pair man from. Some say he is French. Others swear he is Latvian or Finnish. There was a rumour he was from the south of Italy. I think he is from a small independent republic entirely devoted to the export of incompetent young people to the United Kingdom.

'Yes?' he said.

We said we were looking for Alan.

'No,' he said, 'I think he goes to Norway.' We said we did not think he went to Norway. 'I think,' he said, 'if he does not go to Norway, I do not know where he goes.'

He sounded disturbed. But then, au pairs are always disturbed about something.

We only ever had one au pair. She wrote us a touching letter all the way from the north of Sweden: 'I like to wander in the countryside with back luggage,' she said. 'I love also small children and animals, and to be with them in natural surroundings. I think I will be a doctor when I leave the university, or perhaps work with disabled people. I like to help

---

3   During this journey Badger was evicted from two supermarkets, three
    pubs and one shopping mall.
4   Although we spoke to someone at Alan's house I am not sure it was
    his au pair.

those in need.'

An honest version of her letter would probably have read: 'I like to go to Drummond's Bar in Putney with other young people to look for men. I like also to drink a bottle of Dubonnet a day, and to sleep in bed until it is time to gather with other au pairs in the "pub". I like also to break domestic equipment and to push young children out in front of heavy lorries in order to test their reactions. I am very interested to telephone friends in other countries, particularly South America, and I like to smoke, especially in toilet facilities. I do not like to clean things or to be involved in cooking in any way.'

'Ask him,' said JP, 'when they will be back.'

I asked him when he thought they would be back. He said he didn't think they would be back. He seemed to think he had gone for good and left him the house.

'Ask him,' said JP, 'if he thinks he's going to Marlow.'

Marlow was not a familiar word to him. In so far as I was able to get any sense out of him at all on the subject I gathered he was not clear that it was a place. He seemed to think it might be a verb of some kind. After a few minutes of this, I said: 'Will they be back? Ever?' To which he replied, 'I don't think they come back. They gone.' With this Conradian dismissal I replaced the receiver. Neither of us had the heart to go back into the pub. It was curious that, after all my neurotic concern about times and schedules, the river had brought us to the right place at the right time. If Alan kept the original agreement, and there seemed no reason to doubt that he would, we would meet him at Marlow at one o'clock the next day.

JP took the torch. I pulled Badger up from the floor where he was squirrelling something with his nose out of a crisp packet. The three of us went out into the night. We crossed the car park and turned towards the river where lay the boat that we were already starting to think of as home.

# Twelve

*We approach Marlow – We are Three Men finally – Jacob is introduced into the narrative – Alan's attitude to river-going craft – We take refreshment at the Compleat Angler – General thoughts on travel – Alan manages to keep in touch.*

The river from Cookham to Marlow runs in a wide sweep through open fields. It seems twice or three times wider than Cliveden Reach. There are fewer trees, too, on the banks. The sky was as wide as the prairie as, next morning, JP and I rowed up to meet Alan.

Closer to Marlow, where there are houses they are no longer the suburban villas of Shepperton or Sunbury, and, when exposing the ambitions of their owners, do so with the kind of flamboyance I always associate with personal number plates or electrically operated front gates.

One place on our port side looked like a miniature medieval castle but, built out of all too clean modern stone, it had the air of something made up from a construction kit bought from a toy shop. Nothing is quite what it seems when among the wealthy. On another bank a white mansion suggesting a nineteenth-century opulence, a tradition of wealth stretching back beyond Jerome's day, turned out to be a hotel. Brightly painted barges, their roofs dotted with geraniums and busy lizzies, throbbed past us on their way up to Henley.

We came through Marlow Lock at about twelve noon, and moored up river of the lock in the now blazing sun. Twenty minutes later there was a shout from the other side of the river. There, wearing a pair of khaki shorts, a T-shirt and carrying his small son Jacob[1] in his arms, was Alan. He seemed cheerful. In fact I would say he was very cheerful until he saw the boat. 'Is that it?' he said.

We said that was it.

'Where do we sleep?' he said.

'In the boat.'

He looked suspiciously at JP and myself.

'Is this some kind of hoax?' he said. We explained that it wasn't. We explained how the rowing planks were unscrewed at night, how the metal hoops went up and the awning was stretched across it, and how cosy and snug it was inside. I didn't mention the fact that there was also liable to be a noise like a pneumatic drill from the for'ard section.

Alan remained unimpressed. 'We'll have to book a hotel,' he said. 'We can't possibly sleep in that.'

JP's eyes narrowed. He took me a few yards away from the skiff as Alan and his son examined it. They both looked doubtful.

'Once we get him away from his support system,' he said, 'he'll forget all about his need for luxury.'

There was just a trace of the German accent coming back, I thought.

'He will come,' said JP, 'to depend totally on us for his every need. And so we will bend him to our wishes.'

Al was on his knees on the jetty. He leaned forward over the open boat. He wore an expression of solemn curiosity, like a child who is attending a religious ceremony he doesn't quite understand.

'Which way round does it go?' he said.

We explained that from now on he would have to be using words like 'aft' and 'for'ard' and 'stern' and 'prow'. He looked

---

1  Jacob is two and a half years old. He already shows signs of being as authoritative as his father. For instance, when travelling in the back of cars he will often shout 'Go left!' to the driver, for no apparent reason. His father encourages him in this practice.

at us, his big eyes as expressive as a baby lemur's.

'I don't see where we will all fit in,' he said, piteously. Then he crawled on his knees along the jetty, looking down at the conveyance we had lined up for him. His young son followed, also on his knees, looking serious. From the other side of the river came Philippa carrying a small overnight bag. JP led me further away from Alan.

'It is important,' he said, the German accent now even more pronounced, 'to separate him from his immediate family. It is so in the English public school I think. They will try to climb into the vessel. Do not let them.'

Al was now padding back towards us on all fours. Jacob was still padding behind him. They both looked deeply troubled.

'Where are the oars?' Al said. We explained that they were not called oars but sculls. We told him that they were laid length-ways in the boat when the craft wasn't moving. We told him that this was called 'shipping' the sculls. He didn't seem interested. He was looking across the weir at the large white hotel that fronted the calm patch of water immediately before the weir.

'That looks a nice place,' he said. 'We could go there for a drink.'

'Drink!' said Jacob.

That seemed to decide matters. All five of us got into the boat and rowed in a wide semicircle across the river to the hotel. We moored up immediately below a selection of tastefully dressed people sipping expensive-looking drinks on what looked like expensive garden furniture.[2]

'This is ideal!' said Alan.

Keeping a close watch on him in case he should bolt upstairs and check into a double bedroom with bath, JP tied up the boat.

2　The Compleat Angler, Marlow, is perhaps the perfect illustration of how pubs on the river have changed since Jerome's day. Contemporary guidebooks refer to its landlord by name and give a mention to its large black dog. They list, as one of its attractions, 'a dark room for developing photographs'. This was, presumably, the late Victorian equivalent of a jacuzzi. These days, like so many other establishments on the river, it is owned by a company rather than a person.

'One drink', he said, 'and then we must get on the river.'

'Of course,' said Al. 'Of course.'

He looked, I thought, slightly furtive.

JP and I went to the bar and ordered a round of drinks. JP said that he thought that Alan was planning something. He would have to be watched very carefully. I looked out, back through the darkened bar towards the brilliant terrace. In the eye of the gleaming river, Alan was playing with Jacob. The two of them were throwing something to the ground then laughing boisterously. They looked happy.

'Can we do this to him?' I said.

'We must,' said JP.

The five of us sat in the sun. There is a curious feeling about coming to a pub or a hotel by a river. The Viking complex that had afflicted me and JP at Cookham seemed to be getting worse. I caught sight of myself in a mirror behind the bar with two days' growth of stubble on my chin. My cheeks were brick red from the sun, and my eyebrows burnt blonde. I had a strong urge to spit on the floor, to cram my pockets with olives and pistachio nuts and to call, loudly, for drinking horns. Just by our feet, yards away from the weir, rocking slightly in the current, lay our means of escape, strewn with our shockingly public belongings, sleeping bags, rucksack, tents, and, somewhere underneath all that, a two-day-old imam bayeldi from Marks & Spencer. All around us people in blazers and smart shirts, who came here by more conventional means of transport, chatted, drank and nibbled politely, at odds with the landscape.

I thought about D H Lawrence's essay on the theme of *not living where you are*. He listens to two tourists sitting out on a verandah somewhere in Italy, looking at the landscape and talking not of it but of other things. Meanwhile a peasant is working on the hills above them. The tourists are not *living where they are* – their minds are on some things that have nothing to do with the landscape. All around us the crowd, I felt, were not seeing the river that I was seeing.[3] I didn't think

3   Richard Eyre, the theatre and film director, recently gave a classic

you could start to understand it until you had rowed up it. I
didn't want to be on that terrace, sitting by smart people. I
wanted to be back on the boat.

We finished our drinks, bade farewell to Philippa and Jacob,
and in the blazing afternoon, three men, at last, and one dog
rowed up towards Henley.

Or rather, two men (JP and myself) rowed. The dog sat
on the prow, nose twitching, long forepaws draped elegantly
across Alan's luggage. And Alan sat in the steering seat,
beaming.

'This is good,' he said, after a while. 'This is very good.'

Neither of us spoke. We had more or less stopped speaking
when rowing. Alan seemed perturbed by our silence. After
a few vague tugs at the steering line, he got out the mobile
phone from his back pocket.

'Faster, men!' said Alan. It was noticeable that whoever sat
in that seat soon fell under its spell. Shortly he too would be
talking in a German accent. It was also noticeable that, with
two of us rowing, the skiff was moving through the water
much faster. JP and I bent together in rhythm.

Alan looked at the phone. Then he looked at us. 'Would you
mind,' he said, rather shyly, 'if I made a few calls?' 'Not at all,'
we said.

He kicked off with an animated conversation with an answering machine. 'Claudia, hi!' he said. 'I'm on a boat, but you
can reach me on – ' He squinted down at the phone. Then he
looked at JP. 'What's the number here?' he said.

'There is no number,' said JP. 'There is only the river.' Alan
made a face and held the phone up to the light.

instance of this kind of thinking. While on a mountain in Wales filming
*Tumbledown* he was approached by a member of the crew. The
temperature was nearly zero, there was a heavy thunderstorm going on
and the unit was camped on a marsh that sloped down to a nearly vertical
cliff. He assumed the man was about to complain, but, when he asked
him how things were going, the man said, 'Great. I love working here.'
Eyre went on to ask if he liked sub-zero marshlands in thunderstorms,
to which the man replied, 'By here, I mean the BBC.' As Milton once
famously remarked, 'The mind is its own place, and of itself can make a
heaven of hell, a hell of heaven.'

'Anyway,' he went on, 'I'm on a boat. Tell Norman I can't come to LA. I will come, but I can't come now, tell him. I'm on a boat tell him. On – ' Once again he squinted at the phone. It failed to supply the information he required. 'Anyway, I haven't got the number here. But I will call you about Monday.' After he had spoken to Claudia's machine, he spoke to a few more machines. His appetite for talking to them seemed inexhaustible. Each machine, you felt, was an individual, as far as Alan was concerned. He approached them all with the same intensity, enthusiasm and charm. Some of them, I think, were American answering machines.

After he had warmed up by speaking to the machines he called a few people. He got in practice with a bloke called Graham[4] who seemed to be something in the higher echelons of the BBC. He asked him about what time the tennis finished, and what time the film started, and whether the news was going to come before or after a comedy programme, and whether another programme was 52 minutes 30 seconds or 53 minutes 40 seconds, and whether he had trailed the Grand Prix. He seemed to know already the answer to most of the questions he asked. Indeed, there were times when I wondered if he was asking these questions simply in order to catch the man out. But whenever Graham managed to come back with a swift retort or a fact with which Alan was unfamiliar he seemed pleased by the man's independence of spirit. He then asked Graham for somebody called Margaret's number. Then he asked Graham how Margaret was and how her children were and how he (Graham) was. Then he told him, once again, that he was on a boat. Graham, as far as I could gather, seemed impressed with this news.

He switched off the phone then and grinned at the two of us. I thought that this phone call would be enough for him. I was wrong. It simply got him in the mood. He called Margaret and told her that he had spoken to Graham. I got the impression

4  The names, sexes and functions of all these officials have been changed in order to protect myself.

that he was trying to find out whether Graham had rung Margaret and told her that Alan had spoken to him. Once he had established that he was catching the woman off-guard, he started to ask her some of the same questions he had asked Graham. These were mixed in with a few googlies, just in case Graham had managed to get through to her, perhaps even during the course of the conversation, to brief her on the fact that a raving madman was about to ring her up from a boat on the Thames and ask her a series of complicated questions about BBC schedules. He then went on to ask her harder, more complicated questions than the ones he had posed to Graham. What was going to be the exact cost of repeating a programme about China? How long would a certain comedy series, in Margaret's opinion, continue to hold the attention of the public? What were Channel 4 up to? Were they possibly planning a film about China in order to ruin his programme about China? Were programmes about China a good idea? Hadn't we had enough programmes about China? Wasn't China boring? Hadn't we seen it all before?

Margaret did not respond to a lot of these questions. I got the impression she had heard quite a number of them before. He went on to ask Margaret about Graham. They both agreed Graham was working too hard – presumably the poor man spent his weekends sitting by the phone dribbling with fear and wondering from which mode of transport Alan was about to call him next: chauffeur-driven car, train, boat on the Thames, space capsule. He asked Margaret about her children, then asked her why Graham hadn't had any children. He discussed Graham's sex life, in compassionate terms, for some minutes. He described our boat intimately to her. Then he rang off.

'We must find out what the number for this thing is,' he said. 'No one will be able to call me.'

A launch full of people in Edwardian costume ploughed past us near to the port bank. JP reminded us that it was Henley regatta this weekend. Alan's eyes widened. His head jerked up.

'My God!' he said. 'Henley regatta! What are we doing about it?'

JP and I were not quite sure what he meant by this. Did he expect us to have entered for the competition?

'I mean, we the BBC!' Alan went on. 'What are we doing about it?'

JP and I were still not able to answer the question. Alan rang Graham to ask what we were doing about it. Were we covering Henley regatta? Should we be covering it? Was it the kind of thing that people might like to see? I got the impression that Graham was on the point of despatching an outside broadcast unit up the M4 when Alan suddenly lost interest in Henley regatta.

'It's rowing,' he said, shaking his head. 'Do people like rowing?'

JP and I said we did. That was perhaps why, we added with a touch of bitterness, that we were doing such a lot of it. We added that he too would soon be doing a fairly long spell of it. Alan laughed cheerfully. He said he had to make a few more phone calls first.

He went on to call publishers, journalists, restaurateurs, actors, politicians, comedians, agents, novelists and newspaper proprietors. He called television personalities, ballet dancers, architects and film directors. He called singers, theatre directors, sculptors and advertising executives, the owners of new conglomerates, scientists, university professors and fashion designers. He told all of them he was on the boat. He told all of them that he would call them back as soon as he had the number. He seemed, as far as I could tell, to be making a series of arrangements. From time to time as he made these calls, he looked furtively towards us, as if he didn't want us to hear what he was saying. Quite often the word 'meeting' was bandied about.

'Of course,' said JP when he had finished, 'by the time we get to Oxford you will have lost all interest in the phone.'

'Oxford?' said Alan rather squeakily, 'who said anything about Oxford?'

'We did,' said JP grimly.

Alan fell silent. Once again a slightly hunted expression crossed his face. He picked up the phone and toyed with it. But even he had run out of people to call. I watched him with a certain tender solicitude as his big, expressive eyes turned to the scenery – the tiny boats on their way to Henley, the sun now slanting lengthways across the broad river, the green lawns that run down to the water past Medmenham Abbey.

The telephone slipped from his hands and he smiled as he half closed his eyes. The river was working its spell on him. Alan was, at last, relaxing.

# Thirteen

*Evasiveness of Alan about travel arrangements – An incident from his early years – The author's attitude to déshabille – Swimming in the Thames – JP's fearless attitude to immersion – We dine alfresco – Alan's first night in the boat.*

We had never discussed precisely how far Alan was going to travel with us. And, although I raised it once or twice, he was, as he often is, somewhat evasive on the subject. JP said to me when we moored late on in the afternoon, 'If it gets any worse, we can always take the phone off him.'

I said I didn't think this was going to be easy. Alan was sitting a little way away from us, his hand draped gracefully over his knee, gazing soulfully at his only means of contact with the outside world.

Artificial means of communicating with other people have always appealed to him slightly more than face to face contact. Years ago, when he was on his way to an important meeting somewhere, he got stuck in a lift. He was somewhere between the basement and the first floor of the BBC. The alarm in the lift did not respond. A cleaner who was passing on the floor above heard a ghostly voice coming up the lift shaft.

'Hello,' it said, 'hello. Is anyone there? Is anybody there? Hello!'

The man stopped. I imagine he thought for a moment that he was listening to the ghost of some long-dead employee of the place.

'Hello!' came Alan's voice again, 'Hello! I am stuck in the lift! Hello! Is anybody there?' He went on to state who he was, give a brief summary of his career and tell anyone who happened to be out there that he was on his way to a very important meeting. The cleaner, when he had convinced himself that he was not being haunted, was anxious to get help. He spoke, urgently, of firemen and lifting gear. But Alan could not contain himself for long. He gave the man detailed instructions. He told him who he was going to meet, and what he was supposed to say to them. He went on to tell him about all the other meetings he had to go to that day. He dictated memos to the unfortunate man through six inches of steel. He gave him telephone numbers to call and the names of people at the other end of them who had to be given instructions. He told him the precise details of budget plans and strategy documents. By the time he had finished, the cleaner said he felt 'so well briefed he could have run the entire organisation'.

Some people shouldn't be separated from their work. It is sheer cruelty.

Thinking it would cheer him up, we suggested a swim. To my surprise, he removed all his clothes. He sat for some moments, like a centaur in the long grass by the river, his arm draped over his raised right knee like the women in *Dejeuner sur l'herbe* by Manet. I was worried by the political implications of someone as important as Alan being found stark naked by the side of the Thames. What would it do to share prices? Had he put the future of the BBC in jeopardy by this behaviour? A group of people on the other bank seemed to have gathered to watch. Still Alan made no attempt to move towards the water.

I have always been very reluctant to remove my clothes in front of people on whom I do not have sexual designs. It somehow confuses things. I have never been able to be entirely happy when the doctor says in cheery tones, 'Okay, then. Let's get them off and have a look.' It makes no difference that the man has spent his life prodding people in the genitals and shining torches up other people's behinds. One's own equipment is, or ought to be, just that little bit special.

It is the same in swimming pool changing rooms. Quite a lot of the chaps in Putney Leisure Centre stride manfully (in the full sense of that term) from locker to shower, their organs bouncing around like children on a coach trip. They stand under the hot water, scratch their scrotums and say things like, 'Are you going for the BT share offer, then?' I, over in my corner, peering round to make sure that there is nobody lurking behind the lockers, ruler in hand, sneer on lips, wriggle out of my underpants while keeping my shirt low by bending my knees. Then I put my left leg, casually, into my trunks and, with one last furtive glance behind me, go boldly for the moment when the right leg goes up and eyes close to try to brave the awful few seconds when right foot goes into right swimming trunk aperture.

Matters have not been made easier by my children presenting me with a series of eye-catching boxer shorts, which seem to signal to anyone prepared to listen, 'Get a load of this, guys!' They have given me Superman shorts, Deputy Dawg shorts, shorts in the colour of fruit salad, and on one occasion, even a pair that feature an elephant's trunk wrapped over the place where the male member supposedly rests. The worst one features a large sign reading 'Famous Balls' over a picture of Gary Lineker putting one behind the goalkeeper. I am not even really happy removing my clothes in the privacy of my own bedroom. Somewhere out there along the darkened garden, faces smeared with black ink, night telescopes at the ready, are armies of people whose only ambition is to get an eyeful of my John Thomas. I don't think I have got over undressing on the beach at Bournemouth as a child in the fifties. You used to see men and women in what looked like gigantic games bags, striped things that were tied by a cord round the neck, shaking and rolling and heaving as they struggled out of pre-war underwear while my brothers and I dressed or undressed under huge, sand-gritted towels, eyes scanning the beach for nasty men.

JP and Al seemed rather keen on auditioning for the role of nasty men. Both stark naked, they were flaunting their organs at anyone with the time or inclination to look them over. Only after about five minutes did they dive into the water. Clad in a pair of Marks & Spencer's undershorts, I followed them.

JP will swim anywhere. When among the Indians of the Amazon rainforest he never misses getting out of his togs and plunging into the local equivalent of Tooting Bec lido. He seemed sanguine about the possibility of piranha. He laughs at piranha. He claims to find them 'really sweet and friendly' – rather like the snakes that coil round the well at his house in southern France.

I am never sure, when in a river, that some horrible creature is not going to wriggle up from the depths and sink its teeth into my balls. That is perhaps why, if I am going to pee, I prefer to pee with pants on, rather than fishing out the tube with the left hand and paddling away furiously in order to look as if I were not doing anything of the kind.

I swam in a half circle across the stream. Up river, a white cabin cruiser, shimmering on the water like a mirage, came towards me at indeterminate speed.

'This,' called JP, 'is the life!'

When we got back to the boat Alan was somewhat different. He didn't reach for the phone. He sat, stark naked in the grass for some moments. When he was dressed again, he said he would scull.

He sculled rather well. His technique was fussier, more ladylike than mine or JP's. He managed to look, I thought, as if he were thinking about something else, as he wristily dipped the blades in the stream while looking now left, now right, for all the world like someone knitting or toying with a set of worry beads. He even managed to look at the scenery, though once or twice I saw him eye the portable phone in an interested manner.

About four miles down stream of Henley, when the light had started to fade, we pulled in opposite a vessel with a fixed mooring just up stream from the marina. People were sitting out at tables on the deck drinking and eating. I noticed on the side it said it was a floating restaurant and that it was for sale.

On our side, only thirty or forty yards away, it seemed incredibly remote. Rivers, of course, are such natural boundaries. You are surprised to find that people speak the same language on the other bank. JP set up the tent, I put up the awning and Al started to make phone calls.

He had somehow or other found out the number.[1] He rang Graham to tell him. Al said he would be at this number 'unless they try to turn it off or something'. JP reminded him that soon the batteries would be running low.

'We'll have to get some more, then.'

He rang several more people and told them the number. Then he took from his pocket a small box, walked away from us in the gloom along the bank where we were moored and started to fiddle with it. With something like horror I realised it was a very small television. Small, tinny noises came out of it. Alan seemed still to be on the phone to Graham.

'Yes,' I heard him say, 'this is a very good bit. They'll like this bit. Do you think they'll like this bit?' Pure heaven, for Alan, is to be watching a television programme for which he is responsible in mixed company, while on the telephone to other people, all of whom are watching the same programme. In ideal conditions, the people with whom he is watching the programme will also be on the telephone as well. He is working towards the day when the people to whom he and his friends are talking on the telephone are watching the same programme, are themselves on other telephones talking to yet more people, who are watching the same programme while on the telephone to yet more people. One day he will have us all connected electrically in sound and vision, so that the whole world is watching the same programme, and the ripple of gossip about it has spread from London to Karachi, Johannesburg, New York and back across the seas to where it started from.

1  JP had taken the precaution of unglueing the vodaphone number from the side of the mechanism. He had hidden it on a small piece of paper in the bilges of the boat. We still do not know how Alan managed to discover the number.

'What do you think?' I heard him say. 'Do you like it?'

He wandered off further into the darkness. In the distance I heard him call Margaret to ask her what *she* thought of it all. Had she rung Graham? Had Graham rung her? What did Graham say he thought about it all? Was it, perhaps, different from what he had told Alan? Then I heard him call several other people. He telephoned his mother. He telephoned his brother. He telephoned his first and second cousins. He telephoned two aunts and an uncle, and someone in the south of France who might well have been a close relative, but could well have been the head of an important television station. It is often hard to tell with Alan.

By the time JP and I had set up the camping gas and were cooking steak, onions and green peppers fried in olive oil, I saw Alan, who was still on the phone, pacing up and down about twenty yards away, peering back towards the camp fire. He started to wave his left hand like a conductor during a fortissimo passage of a symphony.

'We're having steak!' he was saying. 'And onions! And peppers! Can you believe it?'

JP bit his lower lip. As he set out the plates on the already damp grass, I heard him whisper, 'Tomorrow, he is cooking.'

'Aye, aye, skipper,' I said.

We had been through the German phase, and now I felt we were done with the Viking phase too. We were now probably the core team of a vessel of the old Royal Navy at some time when flogging was still dished out on a regular basis.

'And red wine!' I heard Al say as I handed him a glass, and he handed out our number to more people.

Eventually he came in out of the darkness, and the three of us ate. Badger watched each mouthful go in with fascination and regret. After JP had fried the steak, onions and green peppers we had pork chops and potatoes, fried in the same pan. After the pork chops and potatoes we had neck fillet of lamb and courgettes, still fried in the same pan. With this we ate a loaf of bread, a bowl of cucumber swimming in olive oil, and we drank two bottles of red wine. When we had finished,

Alan rang someone up and told them what we had just eaten.[2] Then we started to drink brandy.

'But this is life, isn't it? Isn't this what life's about, Al, isn't it?' said JP, as we lay on our backs in the long grass, listening to the black river rustle past on its way to where we had just come from. 'All the other stuff doesn't really count, does it?'

Alan patted his stomach. But he didn't phone anyone any more.[3] He put away the phone while we set out the boat for sleeping. JP pitched the tent and retired to it with Badger (who seemed now firmly fixed on him).[4] Then Al and I lay down at opposite ends of the skiff. I noticed that he lay as calm as the Buddha at the for'ard end of the boat, his arms folded across his chest, as if he were rehearsing for the moment of death, like John Donne. And, after he went to sleep, he made no sound. He just lay, peacefully, smiling to himself. The rhythm of the skiff rocked us both to sleep. We did not move until the next day's sunshine was printed strong against the canvas, and the river once again was noisy with launches, steamers, rowing boats, pleasure cruisers and the barges decked with flowers, all beating their way up for the last day of one of the Thames's great summer events – the Henley regatta.

2 Alan addressed these remarks to one of the celebrated chefs in London, Ruthie Rogers of the River Cafe. At some point in the evening, he also spoke to Salman Rushdie's answering machine.

3 JP and I also used the mobile phone on occasion. JP telephoned Scotland where his wife Margaret had, wisely, absented herself. During the conversation, Margaret asked him whether I was intending to write a book about our experiences. On being told that I was, she said, 'Be very careful what you say, JP.'

4 During the course of the journey, Badger and JP formed an alliance even closer than this. At one point, somewhere between Goring and Oxford, JP fed the lurcher an entire packet of thin sliced ham from Waitrose. Badger has never had an experience like this, before or since.

# Fourteen

*Our concerns about Alan – The pure water of the Thames – The question of riparian rites is raised – We discuss travel and anthropology – Deception in the business life – Alan becomes expert at river lore – Ethics of retracing a journey – Does Alan have a dark secret?*

'He's up to something,' said JP to me the next morning. 'I don't like it. He's definitely up to something. He's too quiet.'

He was indeed very quiet, as we packed up the tent and loaded the boat. He spent a lot of time sitting cross-legged by the river dipping the water purifier into the stream.

JP had bought the water purifier at a camping shop. 'With this machine,' he said, 'you can drink water straight out of the sewers of Lima.' He sounded like a man about to buy a plane ticket and fly out to Peru to test this assertion for himself. I said I was quite prepared to drink river water after it had been purified, provided it was boiled as well. Jerome, Harris and George boiled a kettle of river water and only broke off from their tea as a dead dog floated past them.

I simply could not believe that anything bought from a camping shop could carry out a task of any scientific complexity. Alan seemed delighted with the machine. It appeared, as far as I could tell, to have displaced the mobile phone in his affections. He sat, quietly, by the water, pumping up oily liquid into a huge plastic carrier. He looked as if he would not have been out of place in Jacob's play school.

I was keen for us not to get too much river water on board. I

have an entirely unfounded trust in mineral water and, somewhere under the huge heap of junk, old socks, sculls, T-shirts
and sleeping bags, there was a bottle of Perrier – unless, like
the imam bayeldi, it had somehow managed to go to ground
in the bilges.

Just as we were about to cast off, a small, wizened man
drove up to the edge of the river and told us there would be
a mooring fee. JP told him to send the bill to an obviously
fictional address in the Republic of Ireland. The man didn't
seem happy about this, and as we rowed out into the stream,
JP remarked, 'Mooring fees. Damned impertinence.'

As we rowed round the bend the man was to be seen
jumping up and down like Rumpelstiltskin waving a roll of
tickets. It must, said JP, be a thankless task. The poor man
could never really relax. He never knew when some skiff was
going to drift in out of the darkness and get a free night's
parking on his land. He would soon, JP opined, be sleeping
down there, or setting up some kind of hide so that he could
leap out at unsuspecting travellers who were foolish enough
to think that the river bank belonged to all of us.

'The river,' said JP, 'belongs to the parrot-god.' Once he
gets started on the parrot-god it is difficult to stop him. I
sometimes worry that he has spent so much time in mud huts
three hours' plane journey away from the nearest tarmacked
road that he has actually turned into a Tibetan lama or an
Amazonian witch doctor. As he and Al rowed us through the
fresh summer morning, he ran through the creation myth of
his favourite tribe for us. The world, apparently, started when
a crocodile had intercourse with a parrot. After the crocodile
and the parrot had done this to each other, as far as I can
remember, a female giant started menstruating, and during
this period, the tribe (I forget their name now – I think JP said
'they were done by Channel 4 not me') started to eat their own
excrement. When this period in their history was over – we
all felt there were some immediate parallels with the Thatcher
era – they started to eat each other, and when this was over, it
rained for four hundred years. It rained blood, cats and dogs
and, of course, eventually it rained parrots. After this, things

looked up, and the tapir god turned up, had anal intercourse with a few eminent people and ushered in the 'tapir time', a glorious era of manic-eating, coke-sniffing and tapir-bashing which, as far as these demented people were concerned, was a golden age.

I said I thought it was disgusting that public money was being wasted to find out what a group of naked Indians in the middle of an impenetrable forest thought, and the sensible thing to do to such obviously half-witted people was to let them alone. I mean, I said, how can you expect people who believe it rained parrots for four hundred years to make a useful contribution to the twentieth century? Alan said he thought that they were just the kind of people we needed. Raining parrots, he said, made as much sense as people rolling away stones from the caves in which they were supposed to have been buried, or eating holy wafers that were supposed to be the body of the deity.

To my surprise, JP was all in favour of leaving them alone. He said anthropologists weren't the worst things to happen to the Imhaha (or whatever they were called) but, on the whole, it was probably all part of their general drift into nothingness.

We came through Hambleden Lock. Alan said that over on our right we might observe Greenlands, a sumptuous nineteenth-century Italianate mansion in impeccable grounds. It was once, he said, owned by Viscount Hamilton, better known as W. H. Smith. It was now, he added, an administrative staff college.

Something about the manner of his speech suggested to me that he had been sneaking a look at *Nicholson's Guide to the Thames*. He hotly denied this but, like all high-flying executives, he has mastered the art of bluff. I once saw a well-known arts producer go up to a man at the party, put his arm round him, cradle him and take him away from the throng to tell him his latest play was 'passionate, truthful and one of the most exciting pieces of theatre he had seen in the last five years'.[1] When I expressed doubt, later, as to the validity of this

1   The habit of throwing one's arm round the shoulders of someone to
    whom you are giving advice and walking a little way away from the other

view, he replied, 'I didn't see it.'

I once had lunch with an eminent novelist, whose new novel was, as I recall, a book about some people trapped in a hotel room.

'Did you think,' said the novelist, 'that the French character worked?'

I nodded eagerly as he forked prosciutto crudo into his mouth.

'I did,' I said, 'I did!'

The eminent novelist leaned forward and fixed me with a sneer.

'That's funny,' he said, 'because there is no French character in the book.'

I blinked rapidly, and came back with, 'Oh, you said *French* character, I thought you said . . .' 'What?' said the eminent novelist, foolishly giving me more time to think. 'What did you think I said?'

I replied, 'I thought you said the *central* character.'

Over the next two hours the eminent novelist tried, in vain, to catch me out. Although I had only read a five-hundred-word summary of the book, by skilful use of the non-committal remark I made sure the novelist was not able to unmask me. As the lunch went on, the novelist became more and more desperate as he realised that he had made the fatal mistake of *moving too early*.[2]

people in the room has, apparently, been brought to a peak of perfection in the body language of Trevor Nunn, the eminent theatre director. When an acquaintance of mine was working at the RSC at a time when Nunn was in charge of the theatre, this move was universally known as 'trevving'. So widely was it employed that when my friend required Hamlet to impart a confidence to his loyal friend, he simply asked him to 'trev' Horatio. This was then written down in the prompt copy as 'Hamlet trevs Horatio and moves down stage left'. Nunn, who happened to be in the rehearsal room, flicked through the prompt copy and read the words. 'What exactly does "trevving" involve?' he asked, whereupon they all showed him.

2    There is no adequate defence against the skilful bluffer in polite society, since it is almost always possible to evade a direct question. The one simple rule that I pass on to anyone wishing to pass themselves off as expert on, say, the Booker Prize shortlist is, never to pass judgement

Alan has never bluffed on this scale. If he hasn't read something he simply says, with an eloquent shrug, that he has been too busy.

It was noticeable, though, that with his arrival the tone of discussion on the boat had definitely been raised. Pretty soon we moved on from the Imhaha and were discussing the sort of things Alan loves to discuss. The big issues of the day.

'What about the ERM?' he said, his hairy forearms waving expressively: 'What do you think?'

People from other boats, and there was now a positive throng moving up towards Henley, were starting to join in. A man in a straw boater who was punting a group of girls in Edwardian dresses up the river, said he thought it was a disaster for England. Another man, who, it later turned out, knew a friend of Alan's, got on to the subject of art and politics. Soon Alan was talking to almost everyone we passed on the river. They were an increasingly bizarre crowd. They looked like extras for some historical film, or a group specially recruited for some historical theme-park. They were all got out in blazers and boaters, waistcoats, crisp white linen, wide-bodied skirts and the most elegant of trouser suits. He waved at them all as if they had been laid on expressly for our benefit.

'Look at it!' Alan said to us. 'Isn't it amazing! Henley regatta!'

He said this in the tones of a man pointing it out to two visitors from outer space. JP (who has actually rowed at Henley) gritted his teeth, but once Alan has started it is impossible to stop him.

'The first Oxford and Cambridge boat race,' he said, 'was rowed between Hambleden and Henley on 10 June 1829. It is now rowed between Putney and Mortlake. The first Henley regatta was rowed in 1839 and became royal in 1851, with Prince Albert as Patron.'

He wasn't consulting the book as he said this. He had obviously managed to memorise whole chunks of the Nicholson's Guide, and was now regurgitating them, as if he had spent his

on something you have not read or seen until all the other people in the room have done so.

whole life in the place. He went on to tell us that it was the
epitome of an English summer, and the regatta course was one
mile and four hundred and fifty yards long, and that the part of
the river down which we were now travelling was known for
Brent geese. JP, his eyes distinctly flinty, pointed out a group
of birds on the opposite bank.

'Those,' he said, '*are* Brent geese.'

'There,' said Al. 'Didn't I say? Brent geese. You see? Some
of you people don't keep your eyes open!'

We rowed up on the starboard side of the river, past boats
moored up under spreading trees. On the bank, swells who
seemed to have stepped straight out of Jerome's day into ours
poured champagne for their girls. Alan told us that Fawley
Court on the opposite bank was designed by Wren and built in
1684, and that the grounds were laid out by Capability Brown
in 1770. Inside, he said, were various documents relating to
the Polish monarchy and Polish military. We came closer in
to Henley.

On our port bank were hot dog stands, flags, crowds of
trippers, and behind them rows of seats ranged up under
canvas canopies. The scene was almost entirely Victorian. It
reminded me of Frith's *Derby Day*, a huge, animated tapestry
of buying, selling, cooking, eating, drinking, laughing and
shouting, a sensual frieze laid out for us to watch with all the
detachment of a river-goer, one who is only passing through.
Next to the regatta boom, small craft had moored to watch the
next race; in cool silks and linen, they were oddly contrasted
with all that intertwined, baking flesh on dry land. Their boats
were bright with parasols and laden with hampers. They
bobbed on the current as two pencil-thin boats, laden with
huge, muscled men rowed up to the start line in the blazing
July sun. The sun! The sun that was still shining, as it had since
JP and I first went on the water all the way back in Hampton
in what seemed, to me, like another life.

'Note the masks of Tristan and Isolde on the stone bridge,'
said Alan, as JP and I rowed under it. 'And absorb the feeling of
timelessness and Edwardian elegance. You mustn't just grunt
away over your sculls, you know. You must look around you,

as this Jerome man obviously did. Jerome who, by the way?
What was his other name? Osminski or something, probably.'

We said his second name was Jerome. Alan said he wanted
to know his first name, not his second name. We repeated
ourselves. Alan, waving his arms expansively, said that we
obviously hadn't really read the book. Jerome was obviously
not his real name. It was probably a redundant initial like the
K of his middle name. We told him that K stood for Klapka.
He paid no attention to this. As we rowed up to moor a few
yards down river from Hobbs' boat house he became more
and more animated.

'If you're really going to re-create his trip up the Thames,'
he said, as we struggled out of the boat and wandered through
the crowd thronging the wharf in front of the pub, 'you should
do it properly. You should take a tin of prunes and forget the
can-opener like they did. Isn't that what they did?'

JP said it was a tin of pineapple, not prunes. Alan said that
was irrelevant.

'Prunes? Pineapple?' he went on. 'What does it matter? What
does it matter if it was a tin of cannelloni? It was a tin. Right?
Could have been a tin of anything.' His voice was rising in
pitch. People were stopping to look at us as we drifted into
the pub.

'What else did they do?' Alan went on. 'Did they do anything
on this trip? Was open a can of peaches all they did? Is that all
it takes to make an English comic classic? Tell me more.'

JP took me aside as we got up to the bar and ordered the
drinks. He took my left arm and spoke in a low, serious tone.
'He is planning something,' he whispered, 'I know him in this
mood, he has something up his sleeve. Tonight I am going to
take the phone away from him.'

# Fifteen

*I spy a mysterious face in the crowd – A threatening atmosphere develops in the carnival – Mysterious behaviour of Alan – I am visited by aliens – Badger is re-united with a friend and colleague – A sudden influx of strangers – Continued mysterious behaviour of Alan.*

As we came out of the pub I noticed a small man in a neat grey suit. He was wearing a white shirt, a dark tie and highly polished black shoes. What was even more sinister was that, between his hands, he was restlessly moving what looked like a small peaked cap. He had, I thought, the look of someone come to do some vaguely shameful deed. This is how a hangman would look, I thought, checking into a small town, registering in the hotel visitors' book with a false name and waiting in anonymous quietness to do his dreadful business.[1] I walked past him about fifty yards, stopped and, when I was sure he wasn't looking in my direction, took a long, undisturbed look at him.

1  I once met the last hangman in England, Albert Pierpoint, in the hospitality suite of Lime Grove Studios. He was being interviewed about his autobiography, a breezy account of his trips around the United Kingdom in order to string up those convicted of capital crime. Even though most people in the room backed away from him he remained resolutely cheerful, eating large quantities of ham salad. He did not flinch when our researcher apologised for 'keeping him hanging about outside'. I could not even bear to look at him, partly because of my distaste for capital punishment but also out of sheer, primitive dread.

137

He had a lean, hungry face and a pencil moustache. His complexion was ashen, as if he spent too much time indoors; his wide, thin mouth was immobile, and his eyes, large and dark, stared straight ahead of him, as if he appeared not to see the brightly dressed crowds by the water or the bunting that flew in the afternoon breeze. He had now, I thought, the look of a spy or perhaps one of those characters out of the world of ufology – MIBs or Men In Black.[2] His hands, I noticed, had the same deathly pallor as his face. The fingers were long and slender – a musician's hands, perhaps. Or a gunman's. Maybe he was an artist with a high velocity rifle. Perhaps Alan had hired him so that he could pick off JP and me, allowing Alan sole use of all three camping mattresses, unlicensed access to the mobile phone and exclusive rights over the imam bayeldi. Alan and JP came out of the pub. As they passed him, Alan, who was gesturing and talking even more excitedly, did not appear to see him. The man twitched forward slightly and then, as if realising the time was not right for whatever he had to do, coiled back against the wall, although as Alan and JP came over to me he kept his eyes fixed firmly on Alan.

Perhaps he had been sent by another television company in order to end Alan's life well ahead of schedule. There were plenty of people in the world of the media who would be only too pleased to see Alan fail to make retirement age. I myself have heard several other executives refer to him as 'that bastard Alan'. One man, while lunching with me, went on to say that he was 'a swine', 'a ruthless operator' and 'one of the

---

2  MIBs are men in dark suits – Men In Black – who pitch up on your doorstep after you have witnessed a flying saucer in your neighbourhood, and threaten you with horrific consequences if you breathe a word about what you have seen to anyone (a sort of reverse of the technique usually employed by *Sun* journalists on members of the public). What is surprising is that, in spite of the MIBs threatening behaviour, most witnesses hare off to their local ufo-journal and give a detailed description, not only of the saucer but also of the MIBs who tried to stop them talking about it. The conviction that people I am talking to have been taken over by alien beings is quite a common one for me.

most sinister men in the whole of Britain'.[3] Irritating as Alan can sometimes be, I did not want this to happen.

I picked up pace with the two of them and as soon as possible I took Alan's arm and whispered, 'Don't look behind you now, but there's a man over there I don't like the look of.'

Alan gave a quick, crafty look at JP. Then he turned to me. 'Describe him,' he said in a low voice.

I described him. JP, who was standing over by the jetty and looking at the boats, did not appear to be listening. Alan nodded, slightly. Then, his eyes still flickering back between JP and me, he said in tones of surprise, 'I can't think who it might be.'

I'm afraid I had the impression he was not telling the truth. I took a look back at the stranger. He was still standing, motionless, among the holiday crowds, his hat in his hand, as still as a sentry on duty.

'What's up?' said JP.

'Nothing!' said Alan. But I noticed, as we made our way towards the boat, that he was unusually silent.

The second thing I saw as we came up to the jetty was a car, about a hundred yards down on the right-hand side, just before Hobbs' boat house, a Volvo Estate that seemed almost an exact replica of the one outside my house in south west London. All Volvo Estates after a while acquire an individuality – usually a matter of scratches, bumps or dents.[4] Ours is instantly recognisable by its 'Loadmaster' luggage rack, a steel device fitted, unaided, by the author, in Kingston in the early

3  People are always discussing Alan to my face in these sort of terms, with-out apparently thinking that it might bother me. This sort of behaviour is very like people who swear and scream abuse at a car they feel has cut them up only to discover that it's being driven by a neighbour or close friend. They then wave and smile quite cheerfully.

4  The Volvo was my wife's choice. The day we went to pick up the car I sat sulkily in my plastic seat while we completed the hire purchase formalities. My wife informed the salesman, cheerfully, that I had not wanted a Volvo. When we went out to the car we found a large bouquet of flowers in the back seat. The salesman said, 'The flowers are for Mr Williams, in the hope that he gets to like the vehicle.' This joke so won me over that since then I have been completely devoted to the car.

summer of 1992 over a period of about two and a half hours.
This car had such a rack.

In the back of this sensationally clever doppelganger for the
Williams family car was a black and white border collie, who
bore an uncanny resemblance to Fly, the puppy I bought for
my youngest son in the Christmas of that year. All border col-
lies, like Volvo Estates, resemble and behave exactly like each
other, but this particular border collie had a way of coquettishly drawing his neck into his shoulders and splaying his
forepaws on the car boot carpet that made it hard for me not
to think that this dog was one of mine. Unlike Montmorency,
Fly is a real dog; but I have rarely seen him on his own. He was
bought, principally, as a companion for Badger, since neither
my wife nor I could bear the look Badger gave us whenever
we returned to the house, even after a brief absence. Although
some people felt the expression was no different from the one
usually on Badger's pointed face, it seemed to us to be a direct
reproach for our unfeeling absence from him, in order to
pursue the mundane business of getting enough cash to keep
him in bones, dog duvets, leather leashes, wide collars and the
variety of butcher's tripe, dog chox, 'frendlee' dog snacks with
lamb, chicken and beef flavours, and of course plastic bowls
for him to nose around the scullery floor.

Badger has trained Fly well – or perhaps it would be more
accurate to say, Badger as the older, more experienced animal
has corrupted a perfectly good sheepdog. Fly now lies in wait
for him behind bushes and, as Badger passes, leaps out on
him, seizing his neck and hurling him to the ground. But
this is, quite clearly, not an indication of aggression. Badger
has simply trained Fly to do this, very much as Peter Sellers
trained Bert Kwok, his Japanese manservant in the Pink Pan-
ther films, to leap out at him when he was least expecting it in
order to test the speed and strength of his master's response.

I looked through the back window of the Volvo. Then I
looked at the number plate. It too seemed familiar. As I waited,
from out of the driver's door came an attractive, auburn
haired woman in early middle age, who bore an even stronger
resemblance to my wife than did the Volvo Estate to the car

purchased by me from Ian Allen Motors, South Wimbledon.
I was about to comment on this extraordinary coincidence to
Alan when, from the rear door of the vehicle, three youths
in baseball caps (two blue, one red) emerged and stood on
the pavement, hands deep in their jeans, as if waiting for
something to happen.

I was beginning to suspect that some ghastly genetic accident had occurred. Unknown to me, in the Thames Valley, a
group of people were wandering around who bore an almost
complete resemblance to my immediate family. It might not
even be an accident. It might be that I had stumbled on some
low piece of biological engineering, and that perfect replicas
of the Williamses were already circulating through south east
England, waiting to perform some sinister task.

The smallest of the boys, who was wearing a white T-shirt,
blue jeans, suede boots and a hair style that recalled the late
James Dean, was an almost perfect replica of my youngest son,
Harry. In a brilliant simulation of Harry's smile (almost too
shy at first to reach the eyes, and then, briefly and radiantly,
becoming an explosion that wholly transformed his face from
the weary to the cherubic), the creature ran towards me along
the pavement, shouting, just as Harry would have done, 'Nige!'

It became clear to me that we were probably faced with
the first stage of a well-organised landing. Henley regatta was
probably as good a place for these people to start as any, and
the man in the grey suit further back along the waterfront was
probably in league with them. There were probably quite a
few people out there beyond our solar system who would like
to get their hands on an executive as powerful as Alan.

A second boy of about fourteen, blond-haired and blue-eyed,
followed the first creature, heading warily along the pavement.

'Yo!' he said.

'Hi, Jack!' I said, anxious not to offend whoever might be in
charge of these creatures.

'Jack' then put his arm round my waist and said, 'How's
the boat?'

I was almost about to tell him when the third youth ambled
up and offered me his open palm in greeting. Before I had the

chance to take it, he had raised his right leg, whirled round twice, aimed a vicious kick at a point about two yards to the left of me then jumped back to the sort of 'on guard' position adopted by the leading actor of a kick-boxing movie.

'Ned!' I heard myself saying. 'What are you doing here?'

'Alan asked us,' said Ned. 'Didn't he tell you about the picnic?'

'What picnic?'

Then, with the sudden, chilling realisation that these were not simulations from a star system light years away from our own, but my own family, I turned to Alan. He seemed to be in a group of people that he knew. He was standing by the water's edge and talking in the same grand, spacious way that had come over him ever since we rowed in to Henley. He was discussing tennis, television, Bosnia and many other matters that seemed to have little to do with the scene in front of us.

'Al,' I said as he stepped in front of me. 'Alan!'

There was a stern note in my voice, but Alan did not seem to notice it. He steered the man next to him, a character of about sixty in a dark grey suit and smart tie, towards JP and me, and said, 'Do you know Alan Stevens?'

We said we didn't. Alan Stevens, however, seemed to think he knew us. He was sure we had met at Cannes. Wasn't it Cannes? We said we had never been to Cannes. In that case, he said, it was probably New York. I said I had never been to New York. He did not appear to believe this. Everyone, but everyone, he said, has been to New York. Had they? I said I hadn't. He decided we must have met at the Montreux television festival or the Italia Prize at Cortona or the Banff Television Festival in 1991. Both of us maintained we had not been to any of these occasions. JP went on to say that he would not go to them if you dragged him there in chains.

'We're just rowing up the river,' said JP, with traces of his Viking accent. 'We know nothing of what you speak.'

As he said this, a middle-aged man in a slightly lighter suit bobbed up and down behind Alan. His face, I thought, seemed vaguely familiar. He had a slightly weary expression and looked as if he had spent a great deal of time in smoke-filled rooms.

'This', said Alan, 'is Graham.'

Behind Graham came Margaret. I had formed a clear mental picture of Margaret, but like most such pictures it was proved almost entirely inaccurate by her appearance in the flesh. She was a plump lady wearing a brightly coloured kaftan and with the ebullient manners of a barmaid.[5] Smiling, she started to discuss the fact that the Wimbledon men's final was liable to overrun.

'What,' said JP in a grim voice, 'is going on?'

Alan turned to him. 'Nothing, JP,' he said. 'Nothing is going on. A few friends – what could be nicer! A few friends by the river.' From his back pocket he took the mobile phone, and with a look of elation started to dial a very long number.

Graham looked at us wearily. 'He's dialling Morgan le Bone,' he said. Then he raised his eyebrows in a manner of a happily married man registering a complaint about his spouse of many years. 'He's amazing, isn't he?'

He turned to Alan. 'Morgan's in LA!' he said.

Alan, without pausing, cancelled his call and started to dial a new number. Before he had time to dial that number two more men in suits turned up. They introduced themselves as Martin and Tim. One of them was smoking a small cigar. He said something to Alan. I didn't catch all of it, but I did manage to hear the word 'planning'.

At this, JP marched up to Alan, wrenched the phone out of his hand and boomed above the conversation, 'Excuse me Alan. What *is* going on?' He waved the mobile telephone under Alan's nose and thrust his face close to Alan's. 'You're up to something, aren't you? Aren't you?'

Alan's eyes widened in innocence. 'Me?' he said.

'Who is that man?' said JP, pointing at the figure with his

5  These figures, once again, bear no relation to the actual people who turned up at Henley. None of the senior executives at the BBC, male or female, dresses or looks like a barmaid.

back against the wall. The man with the pencil moustache was still staring straight ahead of him twirling his cap between his fingers.

Alan looked at JP. He chewed his lip. He put his toes together. He paused. He put both hands behind his head. Then, coquettishly, he looked up at JP and, in an almost pleading tone of voice, said, 'It's my driver, okay? All right, fellas?'

# Sixteen

*The need for chauffeurs – Lessons to be learned from Jerome – JP reads the Riot Act – Of confidential papers – Meetings discussed – A literary editor's arrangements – Beyond* The Wind in the Willows.

Most senior BBC personnel have a driver. They are, as Alan explained, usually so busy that if they got on the tube like everyone else the whole place would grind to a halt within minutes. JP said it was grinding to a halt anyway. Alan said that was probably because people like JP spent all their time rowing up the Thames and lounging around in hammocks with the Wauru Indians of the Amazon basin. They both got quite heated. Then JP said, 'What I don't understand, Al, is why you need your BBC driver in a boat. Are you intending to give him a holiday?'

Alan said his driver didn't need a holiday. He didn't like holidays. 'Baldwin,'[1] he said, eyeing the man carefully, 'lives

1   Baldwin is not of course the name of Alan's driver. Nor does he have a moustache or look anything like a professional assassin. If I have described him in this way it is simply because at the time the appearance of this amiable, pleasant individual, whose real name is Paul, struck me as threatening. My wife is of the opinion that Paul will probably want to know why I have chosen to portray him as a character out of a novel by Frederick Forsyth. When I explained my motives for doing this she responded, 'He will see it as a hostile act.' It is always difficult to predict how people will react to being described in print. The author of a non-fiction work about a prominent East End gangster, which included horrific descriptions of his killings and betrayals, said that the man's only objection to the book was that the author had got the year and make of

for driving.' I was more interested in the activities of my wife. She was unloading a series of hampers and plastic picnic boxes from the boot of the car.

'Look,' I said, wondering why I was, as usual, both pleased to see her and not quite capable of expressing the fact, 'what's happening?'

She smiled briefly with the air of a woman who does not wish to get involved in a difficult situation, and simply said, 'Picnic.'

She continued to pile boxes, hampers and what looked like a basket full of bottles of wine on to the pavement under the hot Henley sun.

JP was having what looked like quite a serious conversation with Alan. I heard him say things like, 'At least two nights in the boat' in a strict voice. I heard Alan reply, as he pulled at his hair, 'Why though? *Why?*' I heard Alan say, several times, that he was very busy. And I heard JP, indicating the group of people in suits standing by the water's edge, ask what he was busy with. I then heard Alan say, 'Meetings.'

He didn't want to be in meetings, he said. But he was. *This*, he said, indicating the brightly coloured boats, the pleasure steamers and the crowds jostling on both sides of the river, was very *nice*, but . . .

All around us families, courting couples, retired couples and gangs of youths with gaggles of girls were strolling along as if it were the last day of the last summer before the war. I thought of Jerome's words 'let your load of life be light'. The preacher-like simplicity of that thought underlies the whole of his masterpiece. Jerome, brought up in the shadow of nagging worries about money, needed to believe in the simple life almost too much.[2] It is expressed sometimes in patches of

his saloon car wrong.

2  Jerome's pose as an idler ('I love work. I could sit and look at it for hours,') was no more than that. In fact he was a prodigiously hard worker. One of the interesting facts to emerge from Joseph Connolly's biography is Jerome's habit of constantly moving house – usually a sign of the kind of restless insecurity seen in, say, Dickens. This insecurity is fairly evident

appalling purple prose, but when it is the motive force behind descriptions of the little local difficulties that confront the ordinary man it produces great comedy. 'Uncle Podger hangs a picture', the hilarious account of possibly the earliest recorded example of suburban DIY, could be performed, with almost certain success, by a modern stand-up comedian working the clubs. There is a desperate anxiety under the surface of *Three Men in a Boat*. It is a book for us as well as our grandfathers. It is a book, I thought, as I looked at Alan gesturing on the waterfront, about the Toad work and ways of escape from it. As Alan lowered his eyes tactfully and played with the ends of his hair I realised I was looking at a man who *needed* to read this book. Not only to read it: to carry out its instructions to the letter. But I could see that *Three Men in a Boat* had almost nothing to say to Alan. He simply could not, would not, take it on board. Like a woman in love reading *Madame Bovary* or a devout atheist studying the Koran, he could not be reached by it. Our idea of luring him away on a boat to row and row until we reached the head of the river had been a foolish one. He had about as much chance of finishing this journey as Harris did of completing his comic song or getting all those lost souls out of Hampton Court maze.

'What I thought,' I heard him say plaintively to JP, 'was that we could all have a picnic. And then I'll go back to London for this meeting. You see?'

JP said he didn't see. He said he wanted to know what this meeting was about. If it was an important meeting, he said, he would possibly let Alan go to it. But if it was just one of those – he put enormous contempt into the next word – 'meetings', he was going to insist that Alan honour his obligation and come with us up past Pangbourne, Goring, Streatley, Kelmscott and on, on to Oxford whose tall spires beckoned to us across meadows white with the summer heat.

Alan said he didn't know about meadows white with the summer heat. He had no fixed views on such meadows, he

---

in Jerome's autobiography, which drops literary names of the day as if their presence would somehow enhance his reputation.

said. He supposed they were all right; it was the kind of thing that went down well on poetry programmes. But, he reminded us, he had a television channel to run.

'This guy George,' he said, 'in the book, the one who arrived late. Didn't he arrive late? He worked in a bank, didn't he? Didn't they let him go home early?'

JP said that indeed George had met the others at Weybridge Lock, but that once on board he had not been able to ignore his responsibilities. I pitched in here. Hoping to divert the conversation away from real life and back to literature, I mentioned that it was not George but Harris (Carl Hentschel) who, in later years, did not stay true to the threesome. George was loyal to Jerome to the end, I said. JP looked Alan squarely in the eye and said, 'You *must come*.'

He went on to tell Alan that up at the head of the river the Oxford spires were calling us through meadows white with the summer heat –

At this Alan lost his temper. He stamped his foot, rushed over to Graham, opened his briefcase and took from it a sheaf of papers headed CONFIDENTIAL, and TOP SECRET. He waved them under our noses.

'There are forty-three people coming to this meeting,' he yelled. 'And they all expect me to be there! They are coming from all over England. They are coming from Scotland. Some of them are coming from Germany and America. I *have* to be there.'

JP said he didn't care if they were coming direct from the Hindu Kush. He thought Alan should spend another night in the boat.

I must say, this discussion renewed my respect for England's democracy. One could not imagine the head of, say, Pakistan television being told by two scruffs that he had to spend another night sleeping on bare planks in a wooden boat for the good of his soul.

Alan waved the papers furiously above his head.

'Just tell me', said JP, 'what the meeting is about.'

'I can't,' said Alan. 'It's confidential. Top secret.' He waved the papers about some more.

'Can't you read?' he shrieked, 'CONFIDENTIAL! TOP SECRET! They don't just put that on for fun, you know!'[3]

JP and I edged a little closer and tried to sneak a look at the top sheet. Alan held it to his chest.

'Can't you,' I said in a slightly wheedling tone, 'just give us an inkling of what it's all about?'

JP, who had caught sight of a date at the top of the paper, said the meeting wasn't to take place until tomorrow anyway. Couldn't Alan sleep in the boat and have Baldwin collect him in the morning?

'It's public money, JP,' said Al, who was now attracting a number of spectators, many of whom seemed to find him more interesting than the regatta. 'I have a driver so that I can go back to London and have an important meeting with Graham and Margaret and – '

'What I'm saying,' said JP, 'is that the meeting isn't until tomorrow morning.'

Alan looked aggrieved. He spoke as if to a small child. 'This meeting,' he said, 'is to discuss the other meeting. You can't just go into a meeting, you know. You can't just waltz in and make it up out of the top of your head. It takes weeks, months, years to prepare for a meeting. We have been waiting to have this meeting for nearly nine months.'

JP said that a well-run organisation had no need of meetings. Meetings were simply full of people talking a lot of rubbish. Nobody told the truth in meetings, he said; they only tried to impress the other people in the meeting. The only truth you got out of anybody, he said, was by forcing some alcohol down their throat and getting them into a quiet corner where they thought they couldn't be heard. He repeated his demand for Alan to spend another night in the boat. He went on to suggest that Baldwin sleep in the boat with us.

3　For obvious reasons the real nature of this meeting cannot be revealed in these pages. It is, however, perhaps worth recording that when JP finally managed to find out what it was all about he maintained stoutly that it was a complete waste of everyone's time. 'They're only going because they think he wants them to,' he told me later. 'And he's only going because he thinks they want him to.'

'Don't be ridiculous,' said Alan. 'That is offensive and unrealistic and extremely insulting to Baldwin. Does he look to you like a person who would enjoy sleeping on a four-foot-wide boat?'

Baldwin, who had ambled over to join us, said he wasn't really a boat man. He was more an international hotel type of man, he said. He had been on boats but had never really enjoyed being on them.

'You see?' said Alan. 'You see? You see where this sort of thing leads?'

He was getting very much into meeting mode. I rather felt that I was, actually, at a meeting. Alan waved the top secret papers around his head. Some people in the crowd started to crane their necks to get a look at them.

'And,' he went on, 'I have to make about seventy-five phone calls. I have meetings with important people. I have lunches to go to! Drinks to go to! I have to run the show!'

He now seemed quite unlike Mr Toad. Mr Toad, after all, lives in a fantasy land. Alan's fantasy is a strong one, but it is a fantasy that rules all our lives. It is the fantasy that the world of politics and affairs is the real world, the only palpable one.

'Well,' as JP said to me later, when we were discussing him, 'he's basically a good animal. Someone has to do it.'

I thought there was indeed something heroic about Alan, as I have often thought when I have seen him in action over the last twenty years, his eyes alight, his gestures wider and more expansive, as he plans some scheme to save us all, to make everything better. But his dream, quite clearly, wasn't my dream any more. I suppose as we get older that happens.

'Look,' said my wife, 'I've got this picnic. Is anyone going to eat it?'

There followed a long discussion about the picnic. Where were we going to eat it? Should we go and eat the picnic in the boat? Could we hire more boats, possibly motorised ones? If we did hire them, how much would they cost? Who would drive them? Did Baldwin want to row? Where were we going to park the car? Would Jacob like to have a ride in the boat?

I had not realised Jacob was there, but he was. Quite a lot

of new people had also arrived. Alan's brother, Robert, had turned up, and a few of his immediate relatives from Glasgow had also dropped in. A director who was in the middle of making a five-part series for somebody or other had dropped by because he had heard Alan was going to be there and needed to discuss funding. A small man who I think might have been Graham's father was holding Jacob on his knee. Philippa was there as were a couple called Lucy and Alec and a man called Greenberg who was trying to sell somebody something.

I looked around to see if Alan had perhaps invited some of my relatives. Perhaps my brother John had been flown in from Berlin. Perhaps he had arranged for my father to come back from the grave, or for my aunt Kath and uncle Arthur to wing in from, respectively, the West Country and the Charente Maritime district of France. But, before I had even the chance to look, I too was carrying heavy baskets, walking towards Hobbs' boat house while arrangements were being made for the entire flotilla to board motorised vessels (paid for by me) and tow our skiff up river towards Pangbourne. Yet more people seemed to be ordering drinks, although I couldn't quite tell where.

Alan waved his arms, 'Drinks are on Hodder & Stoughton!' Everyone seemed very pleased at this news.

I was beginning to grind my teeth. To JP I simply said, 'Not so much *Three Men in a Boat* as *Twenty-one Men in Three Different Boats!*'

Alan overheard this remark and laughed cheerfully. 'Yes,' he said. 'Indeed!'

He is a great one for organising parties. Or rather, like several other people I know, parties happen around him. I used to know a man called Ian who ran a literary magazine.[4]

4  The literary figure referred to is the poet and critic Ian Hamilton. I have several recorded instances of would-be contributors to his magazine *The New Review* sorting out their artistic and personal problems by talking to each other while waiting for him. There probably should be a coda to Parkinson's Law along the lines of every action requires an equal and opposite inaction in order to discover whether it is necessary

He was endlessly amiable and always asking people to come to see him, especially would-be authors. He worked, I seem to remember, in Soho.

'See you in the pub,' he would say. 'At about twelve.' 'Oh . . . twelve,' I used to say, hoping he would be more specific. 'Sure,' he would say. 'You know . . . twelve . . . ish.'

You would get to the pub at about twelve o'clock and look for Ian. Ian was never there. Instead there would be one or two other shy literary types, several of them clutching manuscripts under their arms. The first time I arranged to meet him, there was a man at the bar whom I thought I recognised. 'Excuse me,' I said, 'are you by any chance waiting for Ian?' 'I am,' he said. 'I was going to meet him about twelve-ish.'

We had a brief discussion about what twelve-ish might mean. Did it mean a few minutes after or before twelve? Had Ian, perhaps, been and gone? We were discussing this when another shy young man, a little down the bar from us, said, 'Oh, it isn't eleven forty-five. I've been here since eleven-thirty. I've come all the way from Colchester to see him.'

We had a nice chat with the man from Colchester. He offered to buy us a drink. By the time we had finished that drink it was about twelve-twenty, and another man opened the door shyly and tiptoed into the pub. He carried what looked like a manuscript and glanced around him as nervously as an adulterer.

'Tell me,' he said to one of us when we had all introduced ourselves, 'would you say twelve-ish meant sort of . . .' Before he could continue any further, I told him that we had had a watch on the pub since at least eleven-thirty. And by the time we had all finished discussing the true significance of twelve-ish a lady poet had turned up from Devon who, too, had been asked to meet Ian at twelve-ish. By now we had bonded as securely as a group of Arsenal supporters on an away game.

or not'. I am not referring here to such trivial activities as not responding to phone bill demands until they threaten to cut you off, but to a more complex use of inaction. I have found in my twenty years' service with the BBC that doing something about a problem nearly always makes it worse. The best tactic is to lower your voice and hope it goes away.

We formed a committee and divided our forces. Some people were set to turning over tables and chairs to see if Ian was hiding under any of them. Some people set out to find his home number, yet others to find his home address. Yet others still were ordering taxis to go around there and find out why he wasn't in the pub. A further group had been despatched to a nearby pub, where somebody said he used to meet people, only to find twenty or thirty completely different people who had all been waiting for forty-five minutes, and were just on the point of sending a search party around to our pub, to see if he was by any chance there.

When he finally did turn up (and he always did eventually), no one was ever able to find out where he had been or what he had been doing. He was greeted by each one of us with the kind of enthusiasm his intimates might have displayed on seeing the Count of Monte Cristo back on the cocktail party circuit. Quite a few of us were in a state of delirium of the kind seen in people who have been queuing all night for a Promenade concert. Often he was practically carried shoulder-high around the pub with a half of lager. Most of the people had, by this time, entirely forgotten why they had come to meet him, or had talked about their problem/manuscript with someone else in the party.

We were now like the people in that Soho pub, a crowd. In *Crowds and Power* Elias Canetti divides crowds into types. I wasn't sure whether we were a mob or a caucus or merely a group with ideas above its status. But, like all crowds, our wishes were patently absurd and often inimical to the individuals who made up our unit. JP, Al and I might have started out as Rat, Mole and Toad but our journey had become more serious, more real. I lugged the heavy picnic basket along the waterfront towards Hobbs' boat house. What was it JP had said at the beginning of our journey? There is no escape any more, not even in the Thames Valley.

# Seventeen

*I am forced to assume responsibilities – Behaviour of the boatman at Hobbs' boat yard – We become motorised – Catering arrangements are discussed – Need for confidently maintained assertions – Effects of alcohol on the company – We prepare to eat the picnic.*

I certainly felt part of the real world. I was in charge of getting the motorboats. The idea was for us to tow the skiff further up river beyond Henley and find a 'nice quiet field'. This was not easy.

Hobbs' boat yard is spoken of in an earlier guidebook as a place 'preparing to hire electric launches from £2 2s a day'. The guidebook makes it sound as if Messrs Hobbs were on the edge of an exciting technological breakthrough, and that being around Hobbs' boat yard Henley in 1889 was a bit like being in NASA the day they first got a man on the moon.

Hobbs' boat yard in 1993 seemed to be in the charge of a depressed-looking man in shorts who was prepared to charge us £30 per boat *for two hour*s. He also had a habit of agreeing to hire these boats to anyone who came along. He hired one to about three different members of our party, some of whom got quite irritable with each other. When we finally got the boat, it seemed to have an engine that might possibly have powered an electric toy train and a steering wheel that was totally slack for the first hundred and fifty degrees of turn and then, suddenly, galvanised into the kind of turning power usually displayed by the

Starship *Enterprise* when making a quick getaway. But, there it is. It was Henley regatta day. Everyone wanted boats.

'Some days,' said Alan, who had mellowed considerably now that we were all doing what he wanted, 'he probably doesn't hire a single boat. This is his big chance with boats. He's made a judgement. He's made a business decision. He thinks he can get that price. He's got it.' He looked at me and gave me a wicked grin. 'Off you!' he said and laughed wildly.

I was hot, depressed and confused. I hadn't really wanted to go on the trip. And now, just when I had started to adjust to sleeping on bare boards and rowing twenty-four hours a day, my family had suddenly leapt out at me and were starting to make their all too pleasant claims.

While I drove the motorboat up river, Harry, as he often does, tried to sit on my knee. Jack was sitting in the back of the boat, absorbed as usual in a book. Ned was exchanging the odd glance of virtually adult sympathy with me. Suzan was sitting next to me. Occasionally when I came too close to the bank she would put both legs and both arms up in front of her face, and give an operatic sob.

'What's this picnic?' I said.

'She's been up since four o'clock this morning!' said my eldest son, gloomily. 'It's performance cookery here.'

She said she had indeed been up that long. She was very happy to make the picnic, she said; she didn't mind making picnics. She didn't mind, she said, getting up at four in the morning to do so. All she asked was that people should just get on and eat instead of running around like a lot of chickens without heads.

'All they have to do,' she said with the passionate scorn of which she is capable, 'is eat it. Is that so much? Is that so much to ask? All I am asking them to do is to sit on a bit of grass and stuff their faces.'

My middle son looked up from his book. 'It's all Alan's fault.'

We agreed on this. Then somebody said it wasn't really Alan's fault but mine. Everyone agreed. Then somebody said it was Suzan's fault for agreeing to make the picnic in the first place. We argued the point. Then someone else said it wasn't her fault but Harry's. This seemed fairly safe ground. It is usually Harry's fault: as the youngest member of the family, he is the easiest to blame. We all agreed it was Harry's fault and left it at that.

It wasn't really possible to get as far out of Henley as we had planned. There was a logjam of boats going up and down the reach immediately beyond the boat house. And the motor launch seemed to go slightly less swiftly than did our skiff, which was now being rowed by Graham and a man I thought I recognised from Channel 4. We also now had two dogs. Badger, who was extremely excited to see Fly, was going through his Bert Kwok routine. I started to shout, impartially, at both children and dogs.

After about 150 yards of this I pulled in (it was a boat you parked rather than moored) behind a large cruiser and Badger and Fly scampered off across the grass. Harry and I climbed out and walked after them, hand in hand.

'Is it nice on the boat?' he said.

'Yes.'

'Can I come on it?'

'Not really,' I said.

I looked back at my family. I realised I wanted him to come. Something was tugging at me. Something was telling me to go home. Perhaps this was what Alan intended. Home is the only place where you can be yourself, I thought, and *all travel is a pretence*. I thought about that character in the Auden poem whose brother was a traveller, and who 'read all of his marvellous letters but kept none'. I thought about Mole in *Wind in the Willows*, how once he got the smell of his own place in his nostrils it was hard for Rat to hold him back. We are defined by our families, not by our friends. Even for those who live long years abroad, one memory of home, one image of a narrow street or a familiar room not seen for thirty years, can seem more powerful than the urgent reality of exile.

The party moved across the grass. I found myself walking next to a woman who, I realised, from the way she was talking, knew me, although I had not the faintest idea of who she was.

The safe thing to do, I decided, was to wait for her to drop some clue. 'We have had quite a journey of it,' she said. This was not very helpful in establishing her identity. I leaned closer.

'It's so hot,' she went on. This wasn't a lot of use either. What I wanted was something along the lines of – 'almost as hot as the lovely island of Crete which is my home.' She did have a slightly foreign accent.

'Jacob is very lively,' she said.

Did this mean she was looking after him? *Jacob is very lively but I have enjoyed coming all the way from Gothenberg to care for him.*' Why are people so cagey in the early stages of conversation? Perhaps because we all know too many people. None of us can remember who anyone is any more. I had just decided that she was a French film star and was working on some opening gambit related to that fact when I realised she was Philippa's brother's significant other.

This business of recognising people is difficult.[1] I was in the Putney branch of W. H. Smith recently, and went up to the manager to ask him whether he stocked an Ordnance Survey map of the Lake District. He seemed, I thought, evasive. When I pressed him on the point, he said, looking at me oddly, 'How are you Nigel?' I realised at this point that he was not the manager of W. H. Smith but a close friend of my brother's wife. I attempted to extricate myself from the situation by saying in a jovial tone, 'Isn't it extraordinary that they don't stock Ordnance Survey maps!'

This manoeuvre only served to make him even more

---

1   I think my difficulties with recognition began when I was returning from Malorees Primary school in the summer of 1956. I saw a tall youth at a distance of about a hundred yards and assumed it was my brother John. I ran towards him, hoping that he would, as he often did on these occasions, seize my hands and swing me round in a circle. I was about to leap up into his arms when I realised it was not my brother John at all. I ran past pretending to give an Indian war-whoop. On another level, it is increasingly difficult for the middle-aged to remember who is alive and who is dead. A friend of mine once asked an eminent poet's widow shortly after his death, how he was. She replied, 'He's with the angels.' My friend, failing to grasp the import of this remark, went on to say, 'Good. And how is he?'

suspicious. He looked at me and said, in tones of gentle reproof, 'Gary'. It was only as he said it that I realised it was his name.

The best way out when placed in this situation is probably to insist that the person you are talking to *is* the Dalai Lama (say) rather than the manager of, say, an off-licence in the Lower Richmond Road. Do not retreat or recant. Once committed to a line, stick to it.

Getting the names of people's children or author's books wrong is a mistake I am so frightened of making that, if I have committed it, I will go to any lengths to clear myself. I remember once remarking to the novelist Peter Prince, 'I very much enjoyed your book *Playground*.'

'I'm glad,' he said, 'although actually it's called *Plaything*.'

'Are you sure?' I said.

He gave me a look not unlike that now being dished out by Philippa's brother's partner.

'I'm pretty sure,' he said. 'I wrote it.'

I shook my head larkily at this news.

'Well, it's funny,' I said, 'I could have sworn it was called *Playground.*' *Playground*, said Peter, was a good title. In many ways, he said, he sometimes wished he had called his book *Playground*. At one stage he thought he might have thought of calling it that; but in the end, he said, he decided to call it *Plaything*. And that was the title. It was his book, he said. He was the author.

'Absolutely,' I said, in a manner intended to suggest that although I was too polite to say so I was still of the opinion that he was unable to remember the title of one of his own books. 'Absolutely. It's your book. You wrote it. You must remember the title.'

I pursed my lips, then looked away from him thoughtfully. 'Although,' I went on, 'it's funny. I could have *sworn* it was called *Playground*.'

I went on to say that the two names were very similar. I wondered whether the two of us had somehow got the two of them confused. Perhaps, I wondered, some editions of the book had been printed with that title, which would explain why I had got the word fixed in my head.'

From the effect of my combative manner I could see I was beginning to get to him.

'That book of Peter's,' I said to a man standing near us, 'is it called *Plaything* or *Playground*?' The person nearby wasn't sure. Neither was the person next to him. Some people said they were sure it was called *Playground*.

'Isn't that funny?' I said. 'I was sure it was called *Playground*. Yet Peter after all wrote the thing, and he insists it's called *Plaything*. But quite a lot of us aren't sure. Isn't that funny?'

Peter said he didn't think it was funny at all. In fact he got quite heated on the subject, but his attempt to suggest that he had perfect recall of the title of one of his own novels was beginning to look decidedly shabby. When I left the party an hour or so later, he was standing in a corner on his own, a grim expression on his face, muttering to himself.

I didn't know half the people at the picnic.

I looked across at the river bank. When Jerome, George and Harris stopped here, before their epic journey back to the boat and the battle with the swans, the weather was cold and miserable. It seemed, somehow, more flagrantly Victorian today than in the pages of Jerome's book. Suzan and JP laid out rugs, trays, glasses and bottles on the close-cropped grass. Then Alan, charging his glass with champagne, stood and proposed a toast. 'To two and a half men in a boat,' he cried. 'And to half a man well out of it!'

We raised our glasses and JP, who had been looking more and more strict as more and more men in suits arrived (Philippa seemed to be on the telephone to someone in a car who was bringing yet more papers for Alan to look at),[2] suddenly relented. He, too, raised his glass. After we'd

2  Senior television executives, like indigent writers, are always being pursued by people with papers for them to sign. At a memorial service for the late Bill Morton, editor of *Man Alive* and subsequently of many distinguished BBC TV arts programmes, a man in mourning approached the then head of Channel 4, Jeremy Isaacs, and whipped out a document of some ten or fifteen pages, bound in clear plastic. I assumed at the time that it was a writ, but was later told it was an idea for a ten-part series about reptiles.

had that toast, I toasted Alan. Suzan loosened the top of the hamper and spread plates on the crisp white tablecloths. She took out cutlery and glasses brilliant in the light of the July day. Then, before our astonished eyes, she began to lay out the most stupendous picnic I have ever seen in my life.

# Eighteen

We ate the picnic. It took one hour and fifty minutes.[1]

1 From the green plastic box she took out several plastic bags. In one was rocket, the peppery leaf popular in new-wave Italian restaurants, although this was grown in our garden. In another, the leaves of a lollo rosso and lollo biondo lettuce bought at the Asda supermarket, Roehampton Vale, washed by her, part dried and stored in the bag that morning. In another, the washed and prepared leaves of a feuille de chêne lettuce with its distinctive red tinge, and in another radicchio which had been given the same treatment. There were mint, thyme and coriander and chives and parsley, all from our garden.

She put these leaves in a large red bowl about three feet in diameter, bought at Emma Bridgewater's pottery shop in the Fulham Road. The sides were thick and solid. She screwed it into the grass with the furious energy that always seems to come to her when she is doing anything connected with food. She put the leaves in the bowl.

From another plastic box she took a bottle of cold-pressed virgin olive oil from a small producer called Abieni near Lucca in Tuscany. She had to draw the cork from the bottle with a corkscrew, as if it were wine, and when she poured the clear golden liquid on to the leaves you could imagine yourself pouring it into a wine glass and sipping it. From her handbag she took a lemon. She put this on a large board (which she took from a red plastic box), and with a large sabatier knife she chopped it in two. She squeezed it lightly over the salad and stirred the leaves with a large wooden fork that she took from the same box out of which she had taken the board.

There was more in this plastic box. Under the lettuce was a prepared cucumber salad. She had made it the night before by peeling and quartering the cucumber, lightly salting and drying it before soaking it in a vinaigrette flavoured with tarragon and dill. Underneath that was a bean salad, made up of flageolet beans, cannellini beans, red kidney beans and English white butter beans which she had bought (loose and undried) from a pulse store in Kingston market and soaked in water a week or so

163

earlier. The beans had been mixed with a different vinaigrette from that used for the cucumber. The oil for this was Filippo Berio's oil from Lucca, to which had been added four or five chopped anchovy fillets. After she had added the vinaigrette she chopped two red onions previously soaked in cold water for ten minutes. Under the bean salad were ten provençal tomatoes, washed and whole. She put these on the board and sliced them with the speed and precision of a sewing machine running along the edge of a yard of curtain material. She put these in a smaller green and white bowl also bought from Emma Bridgewater's shop in Fulham Road and added half a chili pepper thinly sliced with a different knife. She did not add vinegar or lemon to this salad, but poured some of the virgin oil from Abieni, sprinkled a pinch of sea salt and then, from her left pocket produced a pepper mill which she ground, furiously, several times over the tomatoes.

We assumed there would be nothing underneath the tomatoes. We were wrong. In fact we were starting to wonder if the red plastic box had not been keyed in to some tunnel concealed near Henley that led straight to Covent Garden market.

After the tomatoes, she produced three ciabatta loaves (wrapped in foil and still warm), a plastic tub of potato salad (made with new potatoes from Jersey, mayonnaise that she had made herself two days previously by adding the Filippo Berio oil slowly and carefully to the yolk of two eggs, an eggcupful of white wine vinegar, a little mustard and a pinch of salt and pepper), two 'kilner' jars containing tapenade (olive paste which she had bought from Julio's delicatessen in Wimbledon) and home-made rillettes (the recipe for which she refused to give to anyone), one dozen free-range chicken eggs from Sandown organic farm near Guildford and two dozen quail eggs, all of which she had boiled in their shells that morning. All the chicken eggs were brown, wrapped in foil and, like the ciabatta, still warm. She took out, too, a tub of the mayonnaise used for the potato salad, in which, we were told, we would dip the peeled eggs; six green peppers, three aubergines, two red onions, three whole fennel, seven courgettes, half a pound of unsalted Normandy butter, a tub of black olives from Provence, an eight-inch length of Napoli salami, about half a kilo of prosciutto San Danieli wrapped in foil together with a razor-sharp knife for cutting it, and something that looked like a box of cereal. It wasn't a box of cereal. It was a disposable barbecue that she had bought that morning from the Texaco garage, West Hill, Putney. We leaned forward, licking our lips to see what she would do next. Alan, who was kneeling on the grass next to Jacob, slapped his knees and said, 'Well!'

No one else spoke. So he said, 'Well!' again.

Then, as we waited, Suzan went to another plastic box and took out ten red mullet, marinaded in fennel and Pernod bought from Jarvis the fishmonger in Kingston, twenty-four pieces of marinaded chicken and six fillets of best Scottish beef steak, well marbled with fat. She also produced

a large blue frying pan, a medium-sized portable gas stove, about a kilo
of peas in their pods, three more aubergines and two more onions. She
shelled the peas (refusing all offers of help) in about three minutes.
She started to dice aubergines, courgettes and onions very small on the
wooden chopping block. Then she poured in some of the Normandy
butter and an equal amount of the Filippo Berio olive oil into the frying
pan. She put it on the camping gas. Then she put the chopped vegetables
into the liquid that was already turning a warm, yellow colour. They
started to crackle, pleasantly, in the open air. She ignored them. Alan
crept up to the frying pan and started to prod them, but she slapped him
on the left hand quite hard. She then broke six eggs into another bowl
and started to beat them savagely.

'She's making tian!' I whispered to JP. JP nodded seriously and got into
his third glass of champagne.

Having started to make tian, she seemed to abandon the idea. Watching
her cook is a little like watching someone compose the fast movement
of a symphony to order. Just as a theme has been started and seemingly
finished with, another one starts, awakening your expectations in a new
way. It is a process full of delicious beginnings which, it seems to the
hungry spectator, may never be resolved.

She chopped the aubergines, the red peppers, the courgettes, the red
onions and any other stray vegetables she could lay her hands on. Then
she lit all three barbecues, and next to them laid out the chicken pieces,
the red mullet and ten fresh sardines, which she took from a cool box
on the other side of a large wicker basket that I'd been carrying. Then
she took the fifteen white china plates (I was starting to understand why
my right arm ached) and passed them round the huge circle that had
formed around the food laid out on the grass. She poured the beaten
eggs into the frying pan and left the tian to set hard. Only when the tian
was ready, the salads all spread out on a white cloth, the meat, the fish
and chopped vegetables sizzling and spitting on the barbecues, did she
cut it, carefully, into fifteen or sixteen slices and, raising the first slice,
beautifully balanced on a silver knife, say, 'Let's eat!'

After we had each been given a slice of tian, she went to a grey cool
box in which were four bottles of Cloudy Bay Sauvignon, well chilled, and
three bottles of Bergerac Rosé from Henry Ryman. From a wicker basket
next to the cool box were three bottles of 1986 Saint-Emilion. I noticed
that in all the bottles the corks had been withdrawn and then replaced.

'Well!' said Alan again, who was halfway through his slice of tian. 'Well!'

While we were eating and drinking, from a black plastic box on the
other side of the red plastic box, she took a chocolate cake, made to a
recipe from Charlotte, Emma Bridgewater's mother, four tubs of whipped
cream, nine William pears, eight Cox's pippins, figs, dates, grapes and an
enormous cloth-wrapped Cheshire cheese. From the cool box she also
took a bottle of Recioto di Soave, two more bottles of champagne and half

a bottle of Vin Santo, the sweet brown wine from Tuscany. She also took out three one-litre bottles of Coca-Cola, a one-litre bottle of lemonade and two chilled bottles of mineral water.

'That's for the children,' she said.

Then she clapped her hand to her mouth and said in a high squeaky voice, 'Oh my God! I've forgotten the ceviche.'

She seemed devastated by this. We tried to reassure her. We told her there was enough food. We said there was enough food to feed the adult population of Henley for the next three years. But she kept saying it.

'Oh my God,' she said again. 'I forgot the ceviche.'

'What's ceviche?' said Harry. Suzan said it was raw fish and shellfish marinaded in lime. Harry said it was a very good thing she *had* forgotten it. This did not seem to offer any consolation.

'Oh my God,' she went on. 'The ceviche. I forgot the ceviche.'

We talked her down, slowly.

She had left it in the fridge next to the salmon. That was why, when she took the eggs out, she didn't see it.

'Ah!' we said, grease trickling down our chins. 'Ah!'

We carried on eating. We ate chicken, red mullet, steak, potato salad, bean vinaigrette, cucumber salad, ciabatta loaf, and then we went on to chocolate cake and cheese and figs. Suzan gnawed desperately at a Cox's pippin.

'But the ceviche was delicious,' she said. 'It really was delicious.'

We told her we were sure it was delicious. We said it would stay delicious. We said that we couldn't wait to hurry back to London to eat it. We would eat it. We assured her of that. In many ways, we said, it was better that she had left it behind. We had talked about it now for nearly fifteen minutes, we said. It was okay, we said.

Only after her third glass of champagne did Suzan start to recover from what she clearly felt was a major piece of criminal foolishness. By then there was food scattered all over the grass. The dogs were circling us, nosing and sniffing among the ruins of this epic feast. Alan was lying flat on his back while Jacob belaboured his stomach. JP was waving a champagne glass and talking in animated fashion to Philippa's brother's partner. I was beaming fatuously into the middle distance. We were all, like Jerome, George and Harris after their final meal at that private little restaurant in London, 'good and thoughtful and forgiving'.

# Nineteen

*Post-prandial farewells – The parting of the ways? – I am tempted by
the women's hut – Magnificent sternness of JP – Some personal rec-
ollections – Role of father in twentieth-century history – We continue
our journey, with a new crew.*

When everyone had eaten and drunk his fill, Alan and Philippa
and Jacob and Margaret and Graham and Alan's brother
and Alan's brother's wife and the man from Channel 4 and
Philippa's brother and Philippa's brother's girlfriend and the
man with the documents and Baldwin walked or steered back
into the centre of Henley. Then they left us.

JP and Suzan and Ned and Jack and Harry and I looked at
each other.

'Well,' I said. 'Well . . .'

Suzan said it was too late to drive back to London. She was
going to stay at a nearby hotel.

'Good,' said JP, a bright gleam in his eye. 'That'll be nice.'

He clapped me on the shoulder. 'We'd better get back to
the boat.'

I realised with horror that he was serious about this. Suzan
said I would probably like that. Under certain circumstances,
she would have been tempted to join me, she said. Under
certain circumstances there was nothing she would enjoy
more than curling up on the floor of a double sculling skiff.
Just for the moment, however, she said, she had the strange
and unreasonable notion that a double bed with large duvet, a

telephone and a colour television were just what was required.
An iced gin and tonic, brought to her by room service, she
said, would just do her nicely.

'Well,' I said, 'er . . .'

JP pulled his baseball cap over his eyes. 'You're not
weakening, Williams, are you?'

The first sixteen chapters of *Three Men in a Boat* only take
George, Harris and Jerome as far as Reading, immortalised
with the line 'one does not linger in the neighbourhood of
Reading.' The last two chapters only take them up to Oxford
and then back to Pangbourne, where they ditch the boat. I
suggested that perhaps we could abbreviate the journey even
more than the famous trio had done. If we were going to do
the thing properly, I said, we should probably plan to *really*
wimp out in a big way. It would probably be cheating even to
get as far as Pangbourne. In fact, I suggested, to really carry
out this journey in the spirit of Jerome we ought not to have
gone on the boat at all, but sat around in somebody's front
room, puffing on pipes and saying things like, 'I could just do
with sculling up to Maidenhead, old boy.'

JP said, quite briskly, that while on the journey I was not
allowed conjugal rights. He said that among the Hipne Indians
of New Guinea (or it may have been the Atchne Indians of New
South Wales, or indeed any of the bunch of disreputable half-
naked people with whom he spends most of his time), anyone
engaged in a *hoki* or ritual journey such as the one on which
we were engaged was as a matter of course forbidden intercourse with a woman. Anyone disobeying was disembowelled
publicly.

'She must go to the women's hut!' he said.

I said I rather fancied the idea of the women's hut.

'It is boys' time!' said JP.

Suzan said she agreed with JP. She went on to say that, as
far as she was concerned, conjugal rights were not available
to a man who had not shaved, washed or brushed his teeth for
well over three days, and who smelt not only of sweat, mud
and the fabric of the river, but also of stale Marks & Spencer
coronation chicken.

'I could have a bath,' I wheedled.

JP clapped me on the shoulder and marched me back towards the skiff. It looked, I thought, bigger and heavier than it had before lunch. It also looked considerably more uncomfortable. I turned back towards my family, who seemed quite indifferent to my situation.

'We're a man short,' I cried.

I can't remember who suggested Ned should row. I think it might have been Suzan, but I have an idea that JP had a hand in it.

'We must initiate the youth,' he said. 'His body must be decorated with the sap from the wiccaby tree. Then he must eat raw parrot. Then he will be a man. Then he can row.' Lunch, I think, had overstimulated him. He seemed incapable of getting out of character.[1]

Ned said he would like to row. I said I wasn't sure he was up to it. Ned said he was a yellow belt in Kyokushinkai karate, could do forty press-ups with his fingers, sixty sit-ups and stand on his head for hours at a time. He added that he was, in almost every respect, physically superior to me.

It was difficult to argue with this.

I looked at myself in the mirror of the Volvo. My hair was matted, my face sagged with tiredness, my nose, which seemed to have got larger with my time on the river, shone back at me from inside the glass like the Olympic flame. I was wearing a baseball cap with a red checked tea-towel stuffed into the back of it to shield my neck from the sun. The 'Yasser Arafat look,' as JP described it. My shirt, which I had not taken off since we first started on the river, was littered with islands, not to say continents, of sweat stains, and my figure-hugging shorts led down to a pair of knees that had coloured up as if someone had just made them an improper suggestion. The boat was probably the only place for me.

Thinking about baths, shower caps, sewing kits, shampoo,

---

1   JP continued to act the part of an Amazon Indian for the next three hours. We got no real sense out of him until we were about two miles up stream of Henley.

shower gel, large fluffy towels and many other items to be found in the bedrooms of four-star hotels, I climbed back into the rowing seat. Harry looked down at me from the bank.

'Have you seen me enough to put me in the book?' he said.

'Yes,' I said.

'Good,' he said.

Jack looked up from his book. He was sitting on the bank, a little apart from the others. 'Row, scum!' he said, grinning.

It wasn't so bad now that Ned was with us. JP pushed us off with the boathook and we pulled out into the stream. Suzan, Harry and Jack stood on the bank and waved. They waved the way my father used to wave when we'd been to see him up in North London. He would stand out in the middle of the road, my mother standing next to him, and watch the car and wave until we were out of sight. He waved, I seem to remember, not as a farewell but as a way of reaching out across the widening space between us. I rested from the sculls, turned and waved again as we rounded the bend in the river. After they were lost to sight I thought about my father, who will never wave good-bye to me again.

He died nearly ten years ago. He was a teacher and a writer.[2] Although we argued a lot in my twenties, I still can't say his

2   He published one novel, *Agent from the West*, which is a tight and well-written farce, but after that he had little luck with fiction. He left an unpublished novel called, I think, *The Firework Party* which, judging from the few pages I read, illicitly, in his study, wasn't good enough to publish. After his retirement from teaching he wrote several well-received and well-written biographies of Victorian literary figures. One of his briefest and most comprehensible pieces of advice to me, when I told him I wanted to be writer, was 'Write funny.' He certainly tried to write funny. After his death I found a series of letters from the editor of *Punch*. They were rejection letters. They began in a friendly, clubbable manner, often over a page in length: 'Dear David, How nice of you to send me, etc, etc,' and continued in that vein for several lines. As the letters went on they got noticeably shorter, until after about ten or twelve of these the last one stapled to the bottom of the pile simply read: 'Dear David, sorry. No.'

   Oh well, *Punch* too, now, like my father and like Jerome, has received the ultimate rejection slip. A little of me, the part that wants to take revenge, is glad about this.

name without feeling a gear-change in the upper cheek bone
that suggests tears might be on the way. I put this paper
away now, look down at the suburban street below me and
think of his gruff, gentle voice when he came to the hospital
after our second son was born. I think, by then, we were
less self-conscious about touching each other. At least I don't
remember flinching when he put his arms around me, as I had
on Victoria Station some twenty years prior to that.[3]

'It's what you're on the earth for, boy!' he said.

He specialised in these gnomic words of advice. Even
when they were most strange, his remarks had to me the
eerie authority of proverbs. I recall on one occasion him
looking up from the food which we had been served – baked
apple – and saying in a fruity voice, 'I don't like the toenails.
I like baked apple, but I don't like the toenails.' I remember
him coming down one rainy morning, still towelling his face
after shaving. He looked out across the storm-tossed tennis
courts of Mill Hill and said, 'God help all sailors on a night
such as this.'

But he was most at home with the apt quotation – because,
to him, life was lived as much through contact with books as
through contact with people.[4] I remember him when we flew
to Paris together (I was ten or eleven) for what, even then, felt
like a dirty week-end. He tapped the window of the plane (I'd
already asked if we might open it), pointed at the sea and said,
'I think it difficult to believe that Tennyson never travelled by
aeroplane.'

I asked him why. He gave me a line of the poem: 'The

3  I was going to work for six months on kibbutz Kfar Masaryk near Haifa.
    I spent most of my time picking up sticks with the Israeli equivalent of
    the local village idiot.

4  His favourite gambit at the dinner table when I and my brothers were
    being more than usually obnoxious was, 'Je suis vieux et j'ai lu tous les
    livres' – a line, I think, from Lamartine. I asked him after I had heard
    him repeat this twenty or thirty times what it meant, and he said, 'I am
    old and I have read all the books.' I replied that if that was all the French
    could come up with in the way of great poetry, we might as well chuck
    everything into the sea. I think his reaction to this remark was to laugh.

wrinkled sea beneath him crawled.'

I looked down at the water and found it difficult not to believe him. When I was very young he used to walk me to school, since the school of which he was headmaster was close to mine. Before we crossed the main road he would put his hand in mine and sing as we sallied out into the traffic, 'Hold my hand, I'm a stranger in paradise.'

Another speciality of his was asking sudden, frighteningly difficult questions of whatever company he happened to be in. Once on a family holiday in the former Yugoslavia, he fixed the company with a beady eye and said, 'Why did E M Forster take that last fateful journey to Norwich?' No one was able to answer this. None of us knew E M Forster *had* taken a last fateful journey to Norwich. And so, over the next fifteen minutes, ever the schoolmaster, he supplied us with the information that had made the question impossible. Although he never taught me, I think he must have been a good teacher.

On the same holiday, I have a vivid memory of him lying in the shade, asleep, while a large green caterpillar crawled calmly along the bridge of his nose. The caterpillar didn't wake him. He remained as still as someone in the grip of death.

After his funeral, we asked the mourners back to the family home in North London. Although both my father's parents were Welsh (he was a fluent Welsh speaker) our family is not quite Celtic enough to call it a wake. I seem to remember my brothers and me arguing furiously about what wine should be served. Somebody, I recall, suggested champagne, and somebody else said that serving champagne made it sound as if we were celebrating the old boy's demise. What I remember most about the occasion is how I hated the other old people there. One of his oldest friends had the temerity to smile half way through the proceedings. He seemed to me to be glorying in the fact that he was alive and my father wasn't. I am a little wiser now. The ritual meal after the funeral is a way of admitting to the animal in ourselves. After all the pious words, we have to admit that it's good to be able to feel the air on your face, to eat, to drink, to do all the things the one you've lost will never do again.

He was cremated. Someone, I can't remember who, hung on to the ashes. Somebody else suggested taking them somewhere, nobody could quite think where. 'Hendon cemetery is as good as anywhere else,' said one of my brothers. After a lot more debate, we put up a large grey stone. It stands in a section of the cemetery where certain families, mostly Greek Cypriot, have pinned photos of their dear departed to the funeral stones. We thought, of course, that our father's tomb was far more tasteful than that. Chiselled at the centre of a rectangular slab about four feet by three feet, are the words 'David Williams Schoolmaster and Writer'. The man from the cemetery said when we told him we wanted to put the ashes back under the stone, 'You might as well have buried him in the first place.'

I put these memories together to see if they will bring him back, but of course they don't. They are simply a rehearsal for certain moments. I can't join the moments together to make a whole, so that he seems to be moving jerkily, like those pencil figures we used to draw on sets of cards, then flick through to get the illusion of movement.

His last remark to me was as mysterious as almost any other in his repertoire. I put my hand on his in the side room of the ward where he was dying, and said, 'I have to go now. I don't want to. But I have to.'

He looked up at me, his gentle, pale eyes suddenly clear and focused in spite of the stroke and the pneumonia that had followed the stroke. 'In one sense I never want you to go,' he said. And, in one sense, because I believe we should obey last wishes, I never have and never will.

I looked back at the bend in the river that concealed my family, then bent once more to the oars. I was rowing stroke and JP was steering. His pale face was almost dreamy in the evening light. He looked at me and grinned. Then he said, without a trace of any accent of any kind, 'You're devoted to your family, aren't you?'

'Yes,' I said.

Then Ned and I, rowing in time now, pulled on the sculls and the noise of the regatta faded; the tourists and the fake

Edwardians fell astern of us and we were once more alone with the Thames. JP looked beyond us to a point in the stream we couldn't see and I thought, then, that his face was not so much the face of a dedicated traveller as that of some Tibetan holy man.[5] He was seeing beyond our families, seeing shapes in the huge sky behind me as mysterious and important as those patterns his grandfather hauled out of the sun, in Germany, all those years ago.

5   There are times when JP resembles Jerry Lewis in 'The Nutty Professor'. At other moments he resembles a rather distinguished French film star. He has delicate black hair, slightly thinning on top, large eyes and surprisingly sensual lips.

# Twenty

*An encounter with a lock-keeper – Thoughts on officialdom – The
new Third Man – Travellers' tales – A strange encounter near a
lock – I undergo a personal transformation – On towards Oxford.*

The light was going.

A couple of miles up from the next lock we passed a pub.
We were about to moor when JP caught sight of a familiar
uniform.

'It's the same outfit who owned that pub in Cookham,' he
said. 'We must go on!'[1]

We rowed on up to the next lock and moored just down
stream of it near a sign that told us not to do so.

I think they put these signs out just to egg JP on. It was like
a red rag to a bull to him. In spite of my mutterings he tied us
up to a post and in a matter of minutes had decided to organise
an evening meal.

The river's course, as you go further up seems to become
more eccentric. I retraced the journey to this lock later on

---

1  At a later date we went back to this pub, after JP had suggested that
   this book should be a full-scale two hundred and fifty page attack on
   the Beefeater chain. It seemed perfectly inoffensive. On the wall were
   several carefully mounted certificates. These turned out to be awards,
   for cleanliness, efficiency, good humour, tolerance, breadth of under-
   standing, etc, given by senior members of the Beefeater organisation to
   their employees.

from Henley. It took me nearly three quarters of an hour to find it. And yet we had rowed there in what seemed not much more than that. In river time, an hour can pass in a minute and two hours can be as long as a week. The lock was in a pretty, isolated spot, with a steep field just up stream and a weird collection of what looked like caravans on the opposite bank. The flowers had the same well-drilled look you find on most of the Thames locks and the ship-shape lawn seemed to have been trimmed to the same specification. All locks are a curious blend of the private and the municipal, but something about this one suggested the lock-keeper had clearly allowed years of total control over a few hundred cubic feet of water to get to him. There was a sign that said

CANOEISTS SHOULD CARRY CRAFT OVER
ROLLERS NOT THROUGH LOCK.

Lock-keepers can, under certain circumstances, fall prey to commissionaire's disease;[2] some of them are convinced that their real duty is not to river traffic but to the geraniums. I felt, somehow, that a man who could underline a word on a public notice was not to be messed with. He might well not prove as tolerant as the man who allowed me to wolf three-

2  Commissionaire's disease is a condition in which a commissionaire or security man becomes so conscientious about the premises he is guarding that he refuses to allow the people who work there to get into it. It can be caused by many things. Sometimes the sheer effort of asking people to show their identity card and having to give the *impression* that you are matching the photograph to the face, can cause *commissionaire's blindness* in which the subject is totally unable to recognise, say, Bruce Forsyth. It can be caused by *commissionaire's angst*, a condition directly related to the fact that the commissionaire is very rarely called upon to enter the building he guards, although his principal task is to assess other people's worthiness to enter it. Perhaps the most famous example of all of commissionaire's disease involves, not a commissionaire, but a receptionist. The lady performing this function at Bush House, the overseas department of the BBC, was once heard to whisper into her telephone, 'We have a man down here who says he is the Prime Minister of Zambia.'

bean salad only yards away from his sleeping family, and who coped extremely well when he pulled back the curtains to find an empty can of Marks & Spencer's potato salad, a bottle of Châteauneuf-du-Pape and the remains of a half-eaten can of ham and lentil soup all over the edge of his front lawn.

While JP made the evening meal, I looked at Ned. He was sitting at the end of the boat staring out at the river. I didn't know what he made of it all. And I didn't like to ask him. Sixteen-year-old boys, unless there is something seriously wrong with them, do not give you updates on their state of mind. There is something of the terse bravura of a Hemingway character about Ned. I think both JP and I, used to the unbuttoned confidences of early middle age, were slightly shy of him.

He certainly made fewer phone calls than Alan.

Ned's most common response to any piece of news, or any suggestion, is usually one word. Most often he will simply say, 'Mad!'

Sometimes he will say, 'Fat!'

If the suggestion is one of which he does not approve, he may come up with, 'Grim!'

His most commonly used word is 'whatever'. Thus – 'Ned, shall we go to the cinema?' 'Whatever.'

It can be used as a response to almost anything. Statements about politics – ('What's happening in China is terrible.' 'Whatever'). Or domestic arrangements – ('Shall we eat out tonight?' 'Whatever') – are all ground into small pieces by this world-weary, three-syllable adverb, expressing unique disillusion with the world created by the hopeless forty-somethings around him.

He looked at us cautiously as we prepared the boat for the night.

We were tired, and when the three of us finally got into our sleeping bags I was asleep before JP had a chance to start his impression of a tank attack.

I woke to darkness and the sound of a strong male voice somewhere out on the lock-side saying, 'May I come aboard?'

At first I thought this was an unusually polite Thames Valley vandal. Then, peering through a gap in the canvas, I saw that it was a lock-keeper in full mufti. He had got on the peaked hat, the black trousers, the crisp white shirt, the vaguely naval jacket and the highly polished boots. Unless he slept in these clothes (and that, thinking about it now, is perfectly probable), he had presumably dressed specially for this occasion. Perhaps he slept on a watch system to remind him of his old naval days. It was three o'clock in the morning.

There was a pause, and then, having had no response, he repeated his question. 'May I come aboard?' The silence lengthened. Then from the for'ard end of the boat came a decisive voice. 'No, you may not.'

JP is definitely a man to have by you in a crisis. The lock-keeper was clearly not expecting such a crisply formed negative. He was obviously planning an SAS-style boarding attack while we were still trying to work out a satisfactory response to his question. I saw him, out in the moonlight, his trim lock-keeper's cottage behind him, black against the pale night sky.

'Oh,' he said. 'Oh.' He stood to attention then and spoke to the boat as if it were the craft itself he was addressing.

'You are not permitted to moor here!' he said. 'Boats may wish to pass through the lock.'

I saw JP struggle to his feet, his head poked through the awning. 'At three in the morning?' he said. 'Do you think so?'

The lock-keeper continued to stare straight ahead of him. There is, I suppose, no management training course for lock-keepers. They get given a peaked hat or a National Rivers Authority T-shirt and are pushed out into the world to get on with it.

'I must warn you,' he said, 'that you are not permitted to moor here. Boats may wish to pass through the lock.'

This basic ploy – *repeat the bye-laws until the opposition crack* – may have worked on most of the cowed men and women he allowed to drift through his rotten little lock. He did not realise that he was dealing with a man who had coped with everything from mutinous sherpas to violent criminals in the slums of Buenos Aires. JP stuck to the interrogative.

'My question is,' he said, sounding like a man on a phone-in to a prominent politician, 'do you really think any craft are about to pass through your' – he gave a slight touch of disdain to the next word – '*lock* at three o'clock in the morning?'

The lock-keeper stared straight ahead of him. 'The point I am making . . .' he started, then faltered. JP moved swiftly to the attack.

'What *is* the point you are making?' he said.

The lock-keeper averted his gaze. 'You are a danger to shipping!' he said, then, turning on his heels, he went back into his lock-keeper's cottage.

After he had gone, we lay in the boat for some time, discussing the pettiness of those in office. We wondered whether there was a high correlation between lock-keepers and membership of the British National Party. We decided that lock-keeping must be a lonely and frustrating profession. I reminded the company of the story in *Three Men in a Boat* of a lock-keeper who, on being told he was about to be evicted from his cottage, threw himself into his own patch of water. Ned said he thought all lock-keepers ought to commit suicide as a matter of policy. He said, were the lock-keeper to reappear in full dress uniform and hurl himself into the stream, he, for one, would not do anything to stop him.

Then JP started to tell travellers' tales. He told us about his friend in Thailand who owns a sex shop and who had a customer request from him a full-sized rubber doll of a woman.

'My God!' said Ned. 'Whatever did he want that for?'

'What do you think?' said JP. Ned thought about this for some moments in the dark. We all did. Then JP said, 'He wanted one with batteries.'

We started to laugh. While we were still laughing, JP told us how he had had to go into a sex shop and ask for a six-foot battery-operated rubber woman. He went on to tell us that the last remaining dildo factory in the United Kingdom was to be found in the Midlands. Ned asked him to tell us more stories. So JP told us how, on Everest, he had walked to the edge of a crevasse without pitons, and how the expedition leader had screamed at him. Looking down, he realised he was one foot away from a slide of thousands of feet down to endless

snow. He told us about how one of the tribes he had filmed in
the Amazon had killed a man because they thought he was a
sorcerer. I told them about Redmond O'Hanlon's[3] account of
the search for a deep-water monster somewhere in the Congo.

'Yes,' said JP, 'I was offered that.'

I thought at first that he meant that Redmond had asked
him to come with him, but then I realised that these attractions
had become a commodity among hard-bitten travellers. He
seemed to have undertaken them all. He had gone looking
for the yeti in Nepal. He had stumbled across the border into
Burma without a passport. He had been to China, Poland,
Iceland and *yet*, he said, he thought he had never seen
anything quite as bizarre as a man dressing up in blazer, shirt,
trousers and boots at three in the morning asking to 'come
aboard' a thirty-foot camping skiff.

Then we started to laugh again. I thought of the Irish story
of a small farmer in the far west of Connemara who, for some
reason, standing out one fine night on his little patch of land
under the moon, started to laugh. The story goes on to tell how
his neighbour just along the headland heard the laugh, and,
for no other reason than that he had heard it, started to laugh
as well. As so the laughter spread, from small plot of land to
small plot of land, until it seemed as if the whole of the west,
the bachelors, the small farmers, the lonely men who were
left behind after long emigration were all laughing under the
moonlight as they looked out at the wide Atlantic.

I wanted our laughter to spread like that; but England is not
that sort of country. Alone in his little house, the lock-keeper
slept, and we too fell asleep, dozing on until morning, as bright
and clear as the day that had gone before, came over a river
washed free of the regatta, in which there seemed to be only
us and the big shapely trees and the farmland of Oxfordshire.

3   Redmond O'Hanlon, the author of *Into the Heart of Borneo*, is surely one
    of the wittiest travel writers around. I have on several occasions offered to
    accompany him with a film crew, but he has so far resisted the invitation.
    Whether this is something to do with me or the fact that, in truth, he
    never goes to any of the places he decribes (*see* Chapter Ten, note two)
    has yet to be discovered.

Next morning we took the boat through the lock and moored down stream. JP took a roll of lavatory paper and set out for the hills.[4] I didn't like the look of the terrain and made my way back along the bank, crossing the lock to the caravan site. I wasn't sure that this was entirely legal. Badger came with me, tugging restlessly at his lead. Every few yards I'd haul him up in the air, almost a foot clear of the ground, at which he would turn his head in a sudden fit of depression for a few moments before starting the whole procedure all over again.

As I came up to the lock I saw the lock-keeper. I tried to look as if I was nothing to do with JP, but he looked at me with some suspicion. I pulled at Badger's lead and did a bit of gruff, masculine acting in order to impress the man. I meant to suggest I was not to be trifled with. If I could behave like this to a perfectly innocent lurcher, who could tell what I might do were I to be crossed by a power-mad lock-keeper? He was still looking at me suspiciously. I slipped in among the caravans, which turned out to be cabins, marooned in the grass. It had the feel of an upmarket shanty town, temporary, not permanent, an uneasy mix of smartness and shabbiness. It left me wondering whether this settlement was somewhere where people came to escape or somewhere from which trapped citizens were trying to break free.

I moved among these cabins, rectangular pieces of steel set

4   I must apologise for the space given over to defecation and urination in this manuscript, as I know some people find mentioning these things offensive. It is, however, a matter of some importance when confined to a narrow boat for about ten days. JP's method was simply walking into the surrounding countryside. On one occasion, near Cookham, I attempted to follow him. He did not seem unduly worried about this. He turned to me and said, 'Find a ditch and crouch down!'

In the end I was able to find a ditch, on the dividing line between two fields in which I crouched unobserved. In fact, when I looked at the area around, it seemed quite a lot of people had been doing just what I was doing. I found the experience so traumatic, however, that I was physically unable to repeat it until fifteen or so miles west of Pangbourne. Once I had got used to this technique, however, I found I became used to the practice. So much so that when at home I found myself facetiously proposing that I 'do it' in the garden from now on.

out on a grid system among tall trees, aware that the lock-keeper had come into the settlement from the other end. I felt like a marked man. If he could get that upset over a skiff moored on a completely deserted stretch of river, how would he react to a man with a dog trying to get free use of a gentlemen's lavatory to which he was not entitled access? When I found the place, a Portakabin of the same size and shape as the dwellings, I slipped inside and, dragging Badger after me, locked myself in the one cubicle. Badger looked puzzled by this. I forced him to the floor as I lowered my trousers. I was only just on the seat when I heard a heavy tread. It was the sound of footsteps coming up the stairs outside. Then with only a thin plastic partition between us, a stranger was standing in the room, breathing heavily.

He breathed like a lock-keeper, his boots sounded official. I waited for him to speak. Any minute he was going to say, 'You in there. You with the dog. What are you doing?'

As far as I could tell, he didn't seem to be doing anything. Just standing there. Badger started to thump his tail on the floor. I put my finger to my lips. Badger looked up at me reproachfully.

Then, very, very slowly the footsteps started to go away. One step, a pause. Then another step. A pause. Then one more step. Then I heard him clatter down the walkway of the Portakabin.

As soon as I could, I pulled up Badger and my trousers, yanked back the door and tiptoed out on to the grass. I hugged the sides of the cabins as I went back upstream towards the boat, stopping at each intersection and peering left and right to make sure the avenue I was about to cross was clear. I felt like one of those American heroes in the last reel of the picture when they are stalked by the baddies through a parking lot, a forest or a warehouse piled high with wooden boxes. In the end I started to run towards the light at the end of the settlement – running as if all the officials who have ever troubled me, my old headmaster, my only psychiatrist, my driving instructor, yes, and the men who had started all this, the men of the Bradford and Wandsworth branches of the Inland Revenue were all hot on my tail.

There, suddenly, was the boat, green awning half stripped. Next to it were JP and Ned. I thought about the journey ahead. Nothing, so far, had gone as I had planned it. But journeys never do. If I was going to enjoy it I would have to surrender to chance, to do what JP had advised and let the river take me. For some reason I had wanted Alan to come on this trip. I had wanted it to be a journey, like Jerome's, in which three Englishmen re-enacted the rituals of masculine friendship-the incompetence at domestic arrangements, the brave face on physical discomfort and the curious blend of irony and sentiment that passes for conversation among the men of this once important island. But it was too late for any of that. I was here with my son, who has grown up in a world that really does seem to have broken with a great deal of the guilt and the pretension that inspires much of Jerome's comedy. *You cannot step into the same river twice.* Each journey, and each moment of each journey, is different. We have to approach each experience as if it were entirely new. For a writer, that is as much as to say that every sentence should be an adventure. I looked across the river at JP. He and Ned were no more than thirty yards away, but they seemed as surprising and foreign as wild creatures glimpsed, suddenly, on some safari in far-off Africa. JP was standing in the tall grass by the boat with a plate of bacon in one hand. He grinned, and called to me across the stream.

'Okay, Nige?' he said.

'I'm fine!' I said.

# Twenty One

And I was fine.

There is really very little to say about the rest of the journey, except that we rowed all the way. We rowed up through Reading, where we took on provisions at Tesco's, directly next to the river, and JP phoned a trans-sexual prostitute in the Caracas Hilton.[1] We pulled up through Tilehurst and moored opposite a wild-fowl reserve next to a sign that said 'No Mooring'. We rowed up through Pangbourne to Goring and Streatley and beyond Streatley to where the river winds through lonely fields. There were larks high up above us, and as we rowed Badger stood up on the prow, his nose wrinkling in the air, as he smelled rabbits.

---

1  He was phoning the trans-sexual prostitute for business reasons, but the reasons were connected with his business rather than hers. He'd just made a film about this unhappy girl, originally a gay man from the north of Brazil and who was dying of AIDS. The only way she could get to the north of the country to see her mother again was to persuade JP to film her during the closing weeks of her life, which he did. It is a mistake to assume that documentary makers are hard-hearted creatures who film their subjects and then completely forget about them.

185

And we lived the way Jerome, George and Harris lived. Our one thought was the river. There were times when we felt we could have rowed through Oxford, way up to where the Thames gutters out in the fields above Lechlade. That dwindling stream, of course, is the river's beginning. That is the beautiful parallel at the heart of all river journeys. But we didn't talk about it. We were living.

We talked about Alan a lot.

'He's probably in a meeting,' JP said as we idled in the shallows somewhere near an open field.

Once the mobile phone rang (Alan had mysteriously left it behind) but, although we turned over sleeping bags, jerseys and groceries, we were unable to find where it was buried until the caller hung up. When we eventually did find it JP suggested chucking it in the Thames. It didn't ring again.

I wondered whether, perhaps, in the middle of some million dollar deal, Alan had remembered the river, decided to call his old friends, and to ask them whether the water was still running under the boat, and the sky above the river was as clear and blue as when he left it.

JP thought this highly unlikely. 'He's happy where he is,' he said. 'That's what he likes. Each to his own.'

He looked ahead of us and pulled lightly on the rudder line. 'One day,' he said, 'we will steal into Television Centre after a good lunch and kidnap him.'

None of us looked at the guide. To be honest, we didn't care whether William Morris had lived at Kelmscott or what kind of geese were to be seen flying in formation over Iffley Lock. Our holiday – and, by now, it *was* a holiday – like Jerome's book, seemed to improve with the lack of historical detail.

Oxford prompted mercifully few memories of my time in that place. If the town brought back any memories, they were inconsequential ones. I remember the time when Donald (now a respected political journalist) and I performed in a production of 'The Changeling' outdoors in Wadham gardens. The performance was taking place under the windows of Sir Maurice Bowra's rooms. In the middle of the death scene, Sir Maurice's fruity voice floated out on to the night air. 'College plays. Frightfully amusing. Everyone dies.' I told Ned that this was where I had met his mother twenty years ago, walking down the High Street. I told him that she literally had flowers in her hair. He seemed to find this embarrassing.

'Oxford is very pretty,' said T S Eliot, 'but I don't like to be dead.' It didn't seem at all pretty to me. There are shopping centres and car parks where, twenty years ago, there was a cattle market. Like every other town we came into from the river, it had a bloated, seedy look about it – a place given over to our only remaining industry – shopping. *Throw the lumber over, man! Let your boat of life be light, packed only with what you need – a homely home and simple pleasures.* We sat in the gardens of waterside pubs night after night, drinking pint after pint of English beer. Ned developed a taste for Special Brew, which he drank straight from the can, while affecting a Caribbean accent. I looked at the smart new boutiques, the bored faces at the supermarket checkout as we took on provisions and hurried back to the boat. *It is lumber, man – all lumber!* We hugged the river for the rest of our journey.

And, as we rowed, we sang. We sang all Bob Dylan's greatest hits, from the first album down to 'Good as I been to you'. We (or rather I) sang the Highgate School[2] song, a piece of unspeakable rubbish the chorus of which goes,

> Rode Sir Roger Cholmely Oh
> Cholmely Oh
> Cholmely Oh
> Rode Sir Roger Cholmely Oh!

2  Highgate School, whose headmaster, Alfred Doulton, once said to me, 'I have called you here because I think you are going to ruin your life,' had three school songs. 'Rode Sir Roger Cholmely Oh' was by no means the worst of them. There was a Latin one which began 'Sursum corda, sursum voces' and another one which was so bad that not even the headmaster dared persuade the school to sing it. My brother John went to William Ellis Grammar School in Highgate, just at the bottom of the hill near the school my other brother and I attended. The boys there were called 'Elysians', and the school song began: 'Elysians we all would be Rather of use than fame' which the sixth form always used to sing as 'Elysians we all would be Rather of fame than use'.

We sang 'When Irish eyes are smiling'. We sang 'Oh, for the wings of a dove' (or at least the version by Ned which begins 'Oh, for the legs of a frog'). We sang songs where we didn't know the words. We sang,

> Blue moon, you saw me standing alone
> Without a dream in your heart,
> Without a love of my own
> and suddenly there appeared before me
> something something something
> and something something
> and something something something something told
> I think it's something something something something
> and something something because the
> MOON HAD TURNED TO GOLD. (*Repeat chorus*)

We sang hymns. We sang 'Ye holy angels bright' and 'There is a green hill far away' and 'Now thank we all our God'. I sang 'An Die Musik' which I think I do rather well. JP said, as I vocalised the accompaniment, that he could have sworn there was a piano hidden in the bushes near Streatley. I put so much into it, he said, it gave you the feeling you were actually there in the Wigmore Hall. Sometimes, he said, it was as if there were almost too much accompaniment.

We ate out of tins and packets. We lay in meadows. We drank wine at ten in the morning. We found the seafood lasagne or rather 'nosed it out' under one of the rucksacks and hurled it into the reeds at the edge of the stream. And then, one day, still as bright as the first on which we had set out, we came back into Pangbourne, where Jerome and his friends had abandoned their boat all those years ago.

One of the first stories the boatman of Constable's in Hampton had told me when I mentioned I was planning to retrace Jerome's journey, was how Jerome, George and Harris had ended their trip.

'They left their boat at Pangbourne,' he said, 'without telling the boatman.' He sounded quite shirty about it.

It was raining hard when Jerome, George and Harris crept

away to take the Paddington train. But it was brilliant sunshine as Ned, JP and I coasted into the Swan. There is no boat house any more, but you can moor outside the hotel. It's a pleasant, friendly place. No one tried to throw Badger off the premises. The people behind the bar were not wearing uniforms or badges. We rang Constable's and told them the boat was moored outside the Swan.

'There's a mooring charge overnight,' I said, 'but we'll pick it up.'

The boatman sounded amused about this. Later I asked him whether they had charged a mooring fee.

'You don't want to worry about things like that,' he said. The river has its own rules.

Ned, JP and I sat out in the sun. As a fitting end to this nursery epic we had persuaded JP's mum (the daughter of the physicist) to come and take us home in her car.

'We must do this again' said JP.

'Yes,' I said. Ned agreed.

'Get Alan to come all the way next time,' he said.

We nodded, thoughtfully. While we drank beer and waited we talked about Jerome. I'd found an entry in his mother's diary, which he reproduced in his autobiography.

'*December 2nd*. Jerome had his watch stolen. An elegant gold lever with his crest engraved that I gave him on our wedding day. Oh, how mysterious are God's dealings with us!'

A little later on:

'*January 12th*. A very severe frost set in this week. Skating by torchlight in Victoria Park. Coals have risen 8s a ton. It is a fearful prospect. I have asked the Lord to remove it.'

Sitting there, on the terrace over the river, I finally understood why *Three Men in a Boat* is as funny as it is. Jerome didn't have to change a thing. His humour is a tribute to his father's pratfalls and his mother's sublime trust that each new disaster is part of the Lord's plan.

I now know why that quotation from Chapter Three haunted me. It was more or less the cry of every Englishman trapped in the suburban castle which we are all taught to want, to want and dread at the same time. It is the authentic voice of my

father who, when asked by my mother what he would eat that
night, would always reply like a wistful boy scout, 'Oh, bread
and cheese'll do me.'

*'Throw the lumber over, man! Let your boat of life be light.*
*Packed only with what you need – homely home, simple pleas-*
*ure, one or two friends worth the name, someone to love and*
*someone to love you, a cat, a dog and a pipe or two . . .*

*'You will find the boat easier to pull then, and it will not be*
*so liable to upset, and it will not matter so much if it does upset.*
*Good, plain merchandise will stand water. You will have time to*
*think as well as to work. Time to drink in life's sunshine – time*
*to listen to the Aeolian music that the wind of god draws from*
*the human heart-strings around us – time to —*

I beg your pardon, really. I quite forgot.'

Until the deflating punchline, the whole paragraph could
have come straight out of his mother's diary. But, in one
brief sentence, the writer speaks, the small boy that watched
from the corner as his Micawber-like father sank further and
further into despair and financial ruin.

*'I beg your pardon, really. I quite forgot.'*

This is pure music hall, the stuff of stand-up comedy of a
hundred years ago. It gives us the authentic flavour of a period
just out of reach of the tape recorder and the film camera. It
is a voice you hear in the early work of the GPO film units
where, for the first time, ordinary people are given a voice.
It catches their pretensions and their littleness – which is of
course, their claim to greatness. Jerome spoke for the little
people in the little houses, the 'Arrys and the 'Arriets who were
his inspiration and his audience. It is important not to allow
Jerome to become part of the nostalgia industry – boaters,
blazers and cucumber sandwiches – because the people for
whom he spoke and from whom, by default, he came, were
the poor, the unrecognised, the lonely and the unloved.

'He's your perfect subject really, isn't he?' said JP when I'd
been droning on about Jerome for some minutes.

'How do you mean?'

'Well,' said JP, 'the voice of the suburbs. The suburban man
really. Isn't he?'

He looked at me indulgently. The sun winked off his glasses.
Next week he was off to Brazil, the week after that to France.
The week after that to the Himalayas.

'Back to the suburbs, Moley,' he said, with a trace of a
German accent. I heard the sound of his mother's car as she
turned into the car park of the pub. I thought about my house
and the street I live in. I could see, in my mind's eye, the quiet,
unhurried order of it all. 'Yes,' I said, 'let's get back.'

The three of us picked up our luggage and walked
towards the car.